RUFFIAN

Kevin J. Grogan
Foreword by Chris Bayless

RUFFIAN

Copyright © 2022 by 1108 Publications

All rights reserved. No part of this book may be reproduced or transmitted in any form or by any means without written permission from the author.

ISBN (9798421551874)

"For he is the minister of God to thee for good. But if thou do that which is evil, be afraid; for he beareth not the sword in vain: for he is the minister of God, a revenger to *execute* wrath upon him that doeth evil."

Romans 13: 4

Dedication

This book is dedicated to my son, Trevor Montgomery, A.K.A. "The Buzzard." At the age of nineteen, you have already accomplished more in your life than I have ever accomplished on my own. Ironically, my greatest achievement is you.

When you were little, I was so busy trying to be something superhuman I missed moments most families take for granted. Later, when you probably needed more of me, I was unavailable. Not because I was pursuing excellence but because I was reeling from my own shortcomings and paying for my own weakness. Through all of that, you kept your chin down and moved forward. You pushed yourself when I should have been there to guide and still, you came through.

I know most dads are proud of their sons, but I admire mine. I could not be prouder of who you are and can't wait to see what more you will do.

#RLTW

Table of Contents

Foreword	6
Preface	9
Introduction	14
"Fuck you, Do your job!"	17
The formation of S.A.R.G.E.	38
The Feds	42
Temporary F'n Assignment	52
Snitches	59
Tang	68
Buyin' dope	80
A flashbang in bed	94
Specificity	100
By a fucking school? Nah dawg	111
I hate to say I told you so, but…	119
That's what you signed up for…	130
Clearing out what we can	136
Getting sloppy, and that's dangerous…	151
Sometimes, you just have to clean shit up	161
It takes a village	171
Let's be honest	175
It's my right...(of passage)	186
A different way of doing shit	195
Same guys, doing the same thing, in the same place	203
Coming up big	227
Open air gun market	231
Then it happened …	242
The Hunt was on…	258

Foreword
By Chris Bayless

"When you take him to the river, all you got to do is poke about 10 holes in the motherfucker's stomach, believe me he'll sink...he's not coming back up. Only reason people float back up is because gas blows them up. Poke 10 holes in the motherfucker, believe me, he'll stay down with the fishes."

That statement was made between two brothers - violent, predatory gang members - during a recorded undercover meeting with an informant. They were going to dispose of my body in a nearby river. But it was the double cross. They were going to kill me during the robbery of a drug stash house - one less person to split the proceeds. Strangely enough, the way in which this convicted killer described what he would do, after he murdered me, is not all that disturbing in the criminal world. I spent my career going undercover on some of the most violent people you could ever meet. His forethought and predisposition to commit such a crime makes perfect sense, especially when you take into consideration how he and his brother had spent their lives terrorizing and extorting people in their own community.

Kevin Grogan spent his law enforcement career in Savannah, GA, pursuing the same type of violent criminals. As a proactive police officer, and a homicide detective near the end of his career, he saw first-hand, sadly, the pain of those who are ravaged by senseless violence.

In his book *Ruffian,* Grogan shines a light on how politicians and the likes of those in leadership positions, until recently, turned a blind eye to the violent crime and gang problem in Savannah, GA. Denying that your city has a violent crime problem doesn't solve it, it allows it to fester and it becomes worse over time. Grogan gives us a candid look at what happens when politics and weak law enforcement leadership collide. In addition, he exposes the fallacy of such denials and the dangers of believing them. You cannot pretend the evil, which law enforcement pursues, does not exist.

Violent crime is on the rise again across the country. Reducing violent crime and removing violent offenders from a neighborhood is difficult and takes time. As Grogan points out in *Ruffian*, the solutions for success do exist, to include, but not limited to proactive policing combined with a community-based approach. Grogan also focuses more specifically on the symbiotic relationships that must exist between state, local, and federal law enforcement agencies. He highlights the importance of understanding how their respective resources, when focused in specific high crime areas, is the best weapon to combat violence. Grogan shows by example, how the process of engaging violent crime must be consistent, sustained over time, and have buy-in from all stakeholders.

Grogan's passion is from personal experience. He knows that removing criminals from the neighborhood prevents violence and saves lives. It's a crucial element to keeping our cities safe. It is humbling and rewarding when people within these communities quietly offer their thanks in support of law enforcement's efforts. It's the respite they search for and it's the respite they deserve.

Chris Bayless is a retired ATF Special Agent with 30-years of experience doing advanced undercover work in the most violent cities across the country.

Preface

Let me tell you a little about Kevin Grogan. I am a patriot. I make no apologies for it…I love my country and I love my countrymen. Things like our National Anthem, our flag, and our people matter to me. We are all symbols of freedom and in my 47 years of life, I've had the privilege of living in this country, and I wouldn't trade it for anything. I have also had the distinct privilege to wear the uniform of my country and my community.

I grew up in Windsor, Connecticut, a suburb of the capital of Hartford. I grew up around Irish people, Bohemian people, Polish people, Russian people, Puerto Rican people, Black people, Indian people, Mexican people, Peruvian people, Canadian people, African people, and probably more kinds of people without even realizing it. I learned incredibly early in life that people matter. Rich people, poor people, Jewish people, Catholic people, Muslim people…all kinds of people ate dinner in my parent's home. The most lasting of the many gifts my parents gave me was the gift of showing me that I could learn something valuable from other cultures and those cultures would enrich my life. It's a gift that benefits me in my life every day.

I don't like every person I have met in my life. I have seen the best and the worst in people and I have been to places where I thank God every day that I don't have to go back. I am also tremendously thankful that I live in a country where I can say and do pretty much anything I want without being molested by our government. I am also thankful that I live in a country where you can do the very same thing. The fact that we place such value on God-given freedoms and allow them to govern our way of life makes this the most livable country on the planet, in my opinion.

In high school, my brother studied the civil rights movement in this country. My brother, being the way he is, read every notable book on the subject from cover to cover. *Soul on Ice* by Eldridge Cleaver and *The Autobiography of Malcolm X* by Alex Haley, which remains my favorite book of all time, are a couple of the ones I remember. I learned a lot about Bobby Seale and Huey P. Newton. I also learned a lot about John Fitzgerald and Robert Francis Kennedy. They led me to learn a lot about Mahatma Gandhi. I was exposed to several different philosophies on how we should live but the underlying theme was always service to others. I found I connected most with Dr. Martin Luther King Jr.'s ideas on equality and from an early age admired his courage to stand up for what he felt was right. Muhammad Ali has been a major influence in my life also.

I admire the men that I have listed for several things, their courage mostly. They spoke out against injustice, and they gave their lives for the cause. I admired that. The older I got, the more I found that I both agreed and disagreed with many things they said and did. This reinforced the other gift my parents bestowed upon me; they taught me that I can respect people that I disagree with, and that disagreement is healthy and helps people grow.

My concern in 2022 is that we have lost sight of the FACT that it is okay to disagree with people. It is okay to have differing opinions on subjects and one culture can appreciate other cultures' experiences and have empathy for people, without actually having walked in the other person's shoes.

I just want to give you some insight as to who I am and where I come from before you read this book. I also want you to understand, unequivocally, why I am writing this book. In the words of one of my all-time heroes, "Our lives begin to end the moment we become silent about things that matter."

I have used the names of real individuals because of my heartfelt gratitude for many of them, and my disdain for others. I have changed the name of anyone who was a target or the subject of the investigation. I've done this for two reasons; the first of which being I, in no way, wish to glorify criminality or those who engage in it. The second, and far more important reason, is that many of the individuals who we investigated, arrested, prosecuted, and convicted have completed their sentences and the ones that haven't soon will. They have paid their debt to society, and I have no intention of dragging their names into a past I hope they can move forward from. I am sincere in my hope what we did made a positive difference, not only in the community in which we served but in the lives of these individuals.

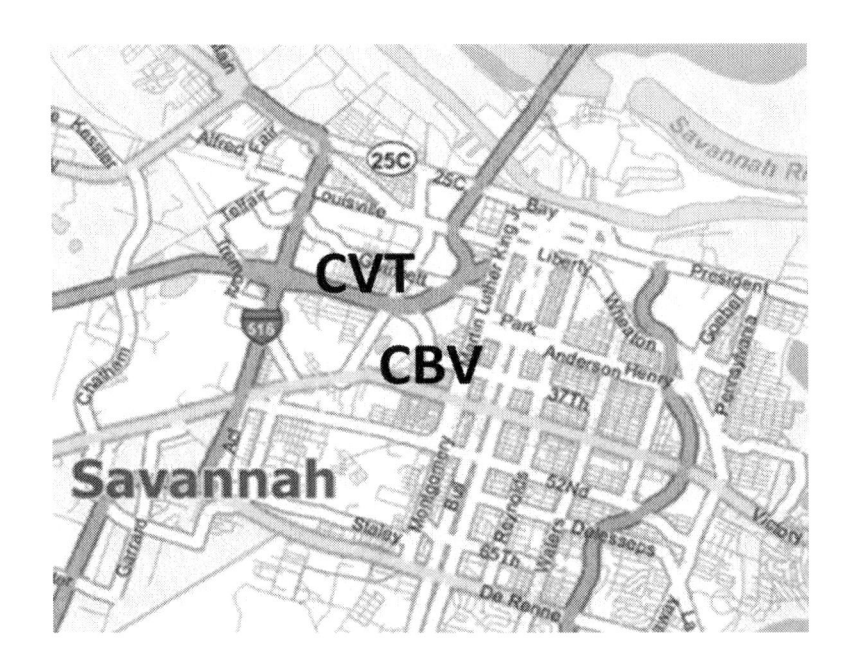

These are the two neighborhoods that the Savannah Area Regional Gun Enforcement Task Force worked in 2010-2012. The letters "CVT" are covering the then named Carver Heights neighborhood and refer to the gang that called themselves the Carver Village Thoroughbreds. "CBV" is covering the Cuyler-Brownsville neighborhood and represents the gangs that went by several different monikers.

Introduction

Ruffian was a Champion. Her heart didn't beat like the other racehorses. She wasn't simply running because she was trained. She was running because she wanted to win. It's all she had ever done and in her four short years, all she did was race and win. She knew nothing else and she wanted nothing else. Her physical beauty was matched only by the beauty of her soul which matched the intensity of her spirit. A dogged determination and unbreakable spirit. She ran until her body couldn't run anymore and even after a catastrophic injury, she was deterred only by anesthesia. Even the medicine could only slow her drive temporarily, she woke, on the floor of the stable and tried to run more, as far as she was concerned she was still racing. No pain, no chemical, not even the fact that she wasn't even on the track anymore could quench her desire to race and win. Ultimately her drive would cause medical personnel to have to euthanize her because she fought so hard to continue she did more damage than they could repair. She was extraordinary, she was majestic, she was a lady and she was a Champion.

We took to this investigation trying to emulate her spirit. A tribute to a long-lost Champion whose determination inspired us to go to work. Neighborhoods had been terrorized by a small minority of criminals. They had made it so citizens who had worked their entire lives to live in their homes peacefully were afraid to allow their grandchildren to visit and play in their yards. This type of living condition in a small community led to one of the most successful federal and local violent crimes initiatives Savannah, Georgia had ever seen.

We launched an aggressive domestic counter-insurgency based on the actions of a couple of juveniles who alerted us to the presence of far more ominous organizations. Guns, Drugs, Murder, Auto theft, Aggravated Assaults, Robberies, and even an illegal nightclub set up in one of Savannah's proudest neighborhoods.

Operation Ruffian began because a few factors aligned. It began because there was a statistical problem that crime was being committed. It began because the citizens were asking for the Police Department's help with drugs in the neighborhood. It began because gang activity was becoming obvious. It was a targeted attack on crime in two of Savannah's proudest neighborhoods, it was not a targeted attack on minorities.

Carver Heights, one of Savannah's renaissance neighborhoods, would become the focal point of an initiative that would lead us into the epicenter of violent crime in 2010, Cuyler-Brownsville. We went at the operation like a thoroughbred after the triple crown with our opposition being the Carver Village Thoroughbreds (CVT) and Cuyler-Brownsville's (CBV) neighborhood gang. We set out to show that without interference and bureaucracy, our tenacity and determination would enable us to succeed. When it was over, Savannah and the neighborhoods where Ruffian would "Race" were safer places.

"Fuck you, Do your job!"

I would wager a guess that anyone who has ever been the police and asked a citizen or potential witness if they saw anything about a crime has heard the phrase, "Fuck you, do your job". In Savannah, Georgia it is almost the rehearsed answer. Now, some people are polite and will tell you they didn't see anything, some just walk away. Anyone I have ever pressed to try to give me information has responded with some variation of those words. "I didn't see shit", "you can't make me testify", "you shouldn't have let it happen in the first place" etc. I sound like I'm complaining but it's just to let you know that getting information, even from people who really want to help is an art form. Society, especially in America today, has made giving police information so taboo that many people don't even know why. If they give information, will they be killed by the perpetrator or their gang associates? Probably not, possible but not likely. Will they be shunned and outcasts in the neighborhood, and have their children bullied? Much more likely.

To me, it boils down to America's lost sense of civic duty. This country was founded on the concept of the greater good. Of the people, by the people, and for the people. Now, I'd be a fool to think that the practical application of these ideals has been purely altruistic and that race, religion, sex, and money haven't tainted the waters but I am, at heart an idealist. Agreeing with Marian Wright Edleman, I think service is the rent we pay for the privilege of living on this earth. I've always felt that way. I knew very early on my life would be spent in the service of others. Over the years I have watched and seen that not everyone feels the same but that there was an appreciation for people who would put themselves between the wolves and the flock. WWII and September 11th, 2001 epitomized America's love of the good guys. Black, White, young, and old all supported our police and military after these events. Probably because the media's portrayal of police was so positive.

Fast forward to 2014 and beyond with stories out of Ferguson, Missouri, Baltimore, NYC, Baton Rouge, Minneapolis, Louisville, and the sensationalism surrounding those cases. Mass media has painted the police as a rogue band of racist murderers.

This country is plagued by a mistrust of the police. In my opinion, it is a misplaced mistrust. I've written about it before and I have argued with people that in many cases simply don't want to hear it. The truth of the matter is that police are human and the overwhelming majority of them are honest and here to help you, no matter your race, religion, sexual orientation, or credit score. In March of 2020, a young lady in Louisville by the name of Breonna Taylor was killed when police executed a "No-knock" search warrant at her home. This created an outpouring of fear and anger in this country and had many calling for the abolishment of "No-knock" warrants. Again, as in the case of Ferguson, Missouri, a public outcry hampered police operations without any investigation being completed or real information. A knee-jerk reaction to a person being killed by police was a result of this type of warrant. The City of Louisville, like many other cities in this country, immediately bent to the will of the masses and banned "No-knock" warrants. I don't bring any of this up to argue the facts or circumstances of the Breonna Taylor case, I bring it up to raise two major points. There is a reason for "No-knock" warrants so banning them outright is foolish and puts police officers at greater risk than is necessary. I also want to remind Officers that perform these duties of their great responsibility to make sure they consider the whole situation, do a thorough investigation and execute these warrants as safely as they possibly can for everyone involved.

It is estimated that nearly 251,000 people die annually from medical errors in the United States. Has anyone called for Doctors to be defunded or the banning of surgery? Or do we realize sometimes there are bad apples, accidents and more importantly, that there is no exact science to the medical profession? There is also no exact science to police work. It's a dangerous business but do we shut it all down because of incidents that end tragically? 1,021 people were killed by police in the United States in 2020, that's less than 1/3 of 1% of our population.

What these critics will never understand, is that the magnification of these incidents and the misinformation that gets spread erodes a sacred trust between police and the community. So, when the police need the community to step up and help in the form of giving information there is always a barrier. It's not new, communities, especially the black community in this country have an inherent mistrust of police. It's grown from the days of slavery, all the way through the civil rights movement of the 1960s into today's climate. For years, however, it was possible to work around. Officers on the street could overcome that mistrust by simply doing their job. Communities tend to trust what they see every day. If a neighborhood has Officers that they see doing their job honestly, every day, A trust gets built.

What's happening in 2020 is that for years, we'll say from 2014 and beyond, these communities have been inundated and bombarded with partial information from every angle. Newspapers and the nightly news were how we used to hear or read about the day's events. Impartial news reports that still had integrity without agendas. Now, newspapers, countless news stations which stream 24 hours a day, social media which we all access through devices that we have in our pockets at all times, report news and opinions that haven't gone through any fact-checking or verification process stream out constantly. This has built an almost insurmountable barrier.

The City of Savannah's city government has come up with a motto, "If you see something, say something". It eats me from the inside out every time I hear it. The main focus of Law Enforcement should be to prevent crime. Yes, also deal with crime after it has happened but safety comes from crime prevention. It's why police patrol, it's why so much money is spent on technology and so many studies are done on trends to deter crime. In the 2019 City of Savannah elections, the majority of candidates ran on a crime-related ticket. Police reform was the main drive of many candidates and cameras outside of the historic district were another. I listened to plans and ideas to get Shot-spotter extended out to neighborhoods near the city limits. My stomach turned as I heard solutions to crime be presented by people who have no idea how to prevent crime. I attended community meetings, where I first met the "New" Police Chief and listened to the propaganda being spread about gangs, guns, and drugs and buzz words but still gave no actual plan to deter, prevent or even moderately lower the crime rate. My disgust grew as I looked back on my own experience and knew all too well what was coming. A Police Chief, with no connection or understanding of the City of Savannah and absolutely no plan for crime reduction, would come to work under a city council who doesn't understand what it takes to keep a city safe. Then City Council has to rely on the Chief that has no clue how to keep its city safe for answers on how to prevent and lessen crime. A Chief that has alienated his entire command staff and Officers into relative inaction.

When the only crime reduction strategy that is implemented is, "We need the community's help" or "If you see something, say something" your city is in big trouble. I've listened to Chiefs over the last five or six years ask for the community's help with crime. Moreover, I've watched Chief Minter get on TV and say the violent crime problem in Savannah is essentially because the community won't help. The thing is if the community has told you, repeatedly, "Fuck you, do your job," then do just that. Just because they won't help you, doesn't alleviate your responsibility to keep them safe. Do your job, police the city.

Technology is a big help for Police to solve a crime. Cameras in high crime or in our case, highly populated tourist areas, Shot-spotter which records and reports accurately when and where shots are fired, Scanners on vehicles to run tags and check for stolen vehicles are all great tools but it is good, old fashioned Police work that keeps cities safe. If crime is recorded on camera, that's great but officers responding will always be too late…when the 911 call is made, the crime has already been committed. Officers who are vested and care about the City, a Command Staff that knows how to implement an effective strategy to prevent crime and a city government in place that will support their Police are a recipe for crime reduction. Operation Ruffian and the Savannah Area Regional Gun Enforcement Task Force (S.A.R.G.E.) was just one strategy that was put in place by some cops who know what it takes to make a city safe using intelligence-led, proactive investigations starting in some of the highest crime areas to identify criminals that need to be removed from the population.

The dope game isn't like regular police work. The hunt is entirely different but terrifyingly similar. The ambiguity is difficult to explain unless you have immersed yourself in this life and even then, everyone has their own style and opinion. If you want to be successful at catching drug dealers you have to be as visible and known as you possibly can, while at the same time being able to sneak up on the most paranoid and suspicious people you can imagine dealing with.

When I rode with EXPO, in bright yellow shirts, with badges shining bright we were as visible and recognizable as any police in the world, I let my presence be known. Just like when I was in my beat in Hitch Village, I was in their face, they knew me and I knew them. When I was in uniform, I wanted everyone I came up against to think that I knew absolutely everything that was going on. The idea, in my head anyway, was that if I could convince them that I knew everything, they would do their dirt outside of my beat. Not the best overall crime reduction strategy but it kept my beat in check. When I worked in plain clothes, the idea was to know more but pretend like I didn't know anything. I didn't want to be seen. I wanted them to do things like no one was watching and keep the same pattern for as long as possible. I didn't even want them to know I was there until I had already gathered enough evidence to make a case. After years of working, I learned to combine the two approaches. I'd approach dealers in plain clothes and because they were familiar with me from being in uniform, they got paranoid that I knew everything. It's a constant head game. Every conversation was a sizing up of what the other one was doing.

Sometime around 2009, my buddy ATF Special Agent Toby Taylor contacted me about putting together an operation in Savannah. I was working at the M.A.C.E. Drug Task Force in Liberty County. Toby didn't need to explain much because he was always trying to do one thing: reduce violent crime. He said he wanted to put together a Task Force that would proactively work with gangs in the Southeast region of Georgia. The thing about the Fed's is they are not responsible for just one jurisdiction. For example, The Savannah Field Office of the ATF covered 54 counties which included cities like Savannah, Brunswick, Hinesville (Ft. Stewart), and Statesboro. After having run and been part of several major initiatives in Brunswick and Statesboro, Toby thought to start the Task Force in Savannah and work their way out towards the surrounding towns. He was looking to start up with two cops from Savannah and see what they could do. When he asked me who he should try and recruit, the answer was easy for me. Josh Hunt and Rufus Brown, the problem was that Rufus had left the department for a contracting job in Afghanistan. I told him Kelvin Frazier was a hell of a cop and he was working in Homicide with Hunt now so he had some investigative experience at this point. I remember being pissed because I wasn't in Savannah. After all, this was exactly the type of operation I wanted to be a part of.

Toby and I had worked on Operation Raging Waters which targeted three neighborhood gangs that were responsible for 40 percent of the violent crime in the city that summer back when I was originally with the Savannah Chatham Metropolitan Police Department (SCMPD). At that point, I didn't have any investigative experience. I hadn't written a search warrant and didn't know how to dig into a major case. I had my ideas but I hadn't done it and nothing teaches like experience. When Toby called and told me he was trying to put it together I had been working narcotics for more than two years, written a hundred search warrants, been involved in three Organized Crime Drug Enforcement Task Force (OCDETF), and had more informants than I could keep track of. I was just wrapping up an investigation that taught me how to put a strong gang case together. I had executed enough search warrants which brought me into the homes of gang members and we recovered pictures, t-shirts with gang names, notebooks, bandanas, and all kinds of evidence. I had learned what to look for and even more importantly how to put it all together to attract the attention of the United States Attorney's Office. If there is one huge benefit to getting the federal government involved in your investigation it's that the sentencing removes the criminal from your environment for a significant time. To me, there was nothing more frustrating as a beat cop than arresting guys who were in constant trouble only to have them back on the streets in a few short weeks or months. It was demoralizing.

Some time passed and Toby was still trying to get things together but hadn't had a lot of luck. I had left the M.A.C.E. Drug Task Force after my Boss, Captain Al Cato (Not to be confused with the terrorist organization) had been removed from Command. In 2010, city officials had made Willie Lovett the Chief for good and I decided to come back home. Well, at least as close to home as I could get from the West Chatham Precinct.

My return to Savannah was exciting for me. A lot had changed but most of the guys who mattered most to me were still around. Josh Hunt was in Homicide, Greg Capers was a Corporal and the Gun Detective in the Savannah Area Regional Intelligence Center (SARIC), Terrance Jackson was back in Central Precinct and several other EXPO brothers were still in town. The biggest omission was Rufus Brown. Brown had left and taken a contracting job in Afghanistan. He had been run down during the Berkow administration and, like so many others, saw a better way to make money. I hated that he wasn't around. Brown and I had always made a good team.

Right before I came back, I reached out to Mike Wilkins. He was a Lieutenant when I left in 2007 but had been promoted to Captain and was the Commander of the Downtown Precinct. As the Lieutenant over Violent Crimes during Operation Raging Waters, he had seen a little of what I could do as a police officer. Captain Wilkins was a good guy. He was always straight up with me and I wanted to get back to my roots. I love Downtown Savannah and it's where I felt I could get back in The Game. Captain Wilkins said he would be happy to have me and he would see what he could do.

Turns out, there were some internal politics I didn't see but my old buddy Greg Capers did. He saw me walking into a shit storm and like he always did, shielded me from it. Detective Capers pulled some strings to get me out to the West Chatham Precinct under the command of Captain Kerry Thomas. It was a blessing in disguise and I figured as long as I was back on the street, I could make things happen. Say what you want but everyone needs someone to look out for them. Capers opened a lot of doors for me in my career and every time he did. I bust through them with everything I had. I never wanted to be the one that made people look bad and hell, I didn't want to look bad either. Police work is very unforgiving. Especially in the Savannah Chatham

Metropolitan Police Department. There was always an air of "What have you done for me lately" lingering. I think that is what made guys like Willie Lovett, Greg Capers, Devon Adams, Rob Gavin, George Gundich, H. Lindsey Rowse and Greg Ernst who they were, they never forgot what you did for them and when you needed them, they always remembered and did what they could for you. It's also what drove me to succeed. I was always looking to do more than I did yesterday.

I got back to SCMPD and was assigned to A watch. Swing shifts worked a month of day shift and then a month of Midnight shift and alternated back and forth. I had been there for a little over a month, done a day shift, and rode with a training officer for a day before my Sergeants decided I could hack it back on the road. It had been a little over three years since I had been on patrol in good ol' Savannah but I hadn't been away from police work. Investigations are a lot different than working the road on Patrol. Investigations, especially narcotics allow you a lot of freedom in your day to do what you have to but it also is pretty lax on the structure. Lunchtimes, break times, exactly what you are doing is much less stringent because supervisors don't have to worry about covering beats while one unit is on lunch, etc. I had been working dope and doing my own thing for three years so a thirty-minute lunch break and making sure I was in my beat was a little restrictive to come back to but hey, that's the job and I fucking loved this job. It wasn't hard to get used to either. Like riding a bike, once I was back in a marked unit things came right back to me. Driving through neighborhoods at speeds where I could see what was going on. Focusing on details that might lead to a stop and making mental notes of who and where everyone was and when they were there. Like clockwork, my head was just back in patrol mode. Now I had some experience. I could now see a little further than I used to. I focused on different things. Tattoos, graffiti, t-shirts, and different activities now had a whole different meaning to me.

So, because I was "the new guy" and just coming back to a watch, I was kind of a rover. If there was an open beat, I got stuck there. Guys who had been on the watch for a while are assigned permanent beats. Guys like Gene Johnson, an old-school veteran had his beat, Daryl Cone was out in Berwick, Tony Edwards was in Georgetown, Sean Horton was back from Forensics and Tupac had his beat on the outskirts of the county where he couldn't bother too many people. The young guy, Kyle Godfrey was assigned beat 13. Carver Heights.

When I got back I knew a bunch of the guys/girls. There were a few veterans that I knew. Not well and no one I had worked closely with but I was familiar and perfectly comfortable with. There were also some young guns and Godfrey by far was the standout. I'd listen out for him on the radio and invariably he'd be out doing something. I liked that. My kind of cop. Russ Champion was also a guy who was bouncing from beat to beat and he showed up a lot too. Godfrey's beat was next to Gene Johnson's beat so when I arrived to back him up on whatever he was doing, Gene was either there or in the area. Corporal Johnson wasn't a spotlight kind of guy. He didn't like a lot of noise or excitement but man, he was always there if he was needed. He was a great guy to bounce things off of because he had been around and is a sharp Officer.

I would dip in, when Godfrey wasn't there and try to cover beat 13 on his days off. My policing style was much better suited for a city neighborhood than it was for the county beats…man, I hated being out there. I always say, wherever you have people, you have trouble and I stand by it. I just didn't like spending long periods in between seeing people. I had worked in Carver Heights when I was on EXPO so I knew a lot was going on there. There had also been an Officer-involved shooting there within the last year where an Officer chased a guy into a house and the guy tried to cut him with a knife. The shooting and subsequent death of the Caver Village resident got a lot of attention and did nothing to improve community/police relations.

The first months I was back, I tried to spend as much time in Carver Heights or Cloverdale as possible. I drove around and started to see everything. Then, the call came in. It was a damage to property call. An elderly woman called in and reported that some juveniles had thrown a rock and broken a window in her home. She lived there with her middle-aged, handicapped son. She told me the story of the puppy she had bought for her son and how he sat behind the fence, playing with his dog. I was infuriated. They wanted the Pitbull puppy and when the helpless man wouldn't give it up they damaged their home and disrespected their vehicle by pouring ketchup and mustard packets on it. I didn't know the neighborhood like I used to know the projects. When the youngin's stepped out of line, I knew who to talk to and keep things unofficial. This was a whole different place. A Neighborhood but not like the projects where I met everyone walking around. Too much ground to cover. It would take me some time to get to know this place but I would start at this corner.

As I took the information for the damage I stood at the corner of Winburn and Wexler. Right on the corner where this incident occurred, there was a roll call painted right on the street. A roll call is a list of people who have died, most especially been killed, and most times, it had to do with gangs. All the telltale signs were there. The roll call list graffitied on the street read TIP (Thug in Peace): H.B., T.P., Bossy, Scooter. I had no idea who any of these guys were but I was going to find out. My initial thought was that whoever threw the rock and painted the 26-year-old minivan in condiments, were juveniles but the roll call, right on the spot where it all happened, was a little more ominous.

I cleared the call and gave the woman a case report number. I didn't go directly to a spot to write the report as most of the time I would do when no calls were backing up. I rode around the neighborhood and started focusing on a whole different world. Tags of "V.B.S" and

"C.V.T." were all over the neighborhood. In the street, on benches in the two parks, on basketball courts, etc. There were these monikers everywhere. Exactly the kind of things I knew all about after operations like Raging Waters and Invisible Fence.

I learned how to police in Hitch Village. A rough public housing project on the east side of Savannah. I saw similar graffiti there which read "HVP/HVC for Hitch Village Posse or Hitch Village Committee. The graffiti in Carver Heights, formerly known as Carver Village, was similar but spread out over a larger neighborhood. Hell, as I drove around Carver Heights, I would see a few HVP tags which I chalked up to the fact that Hitch Village had been torn down and some of the residents moved out this way. Nothing unusual as far as gangs in Savannah go. In Savannah, neighborhoods are king.

There was not a huge difference in time between my days in Hitch Village and now but digital cameras and cell phone cameras had advanced and started to make it a lot easier for me to document things. I started snapping photos of graffiti and of some people hanging out wearing t-shirts that had "CVT" and "RIP HB" or "RIP TP" on them. I was just getting started. Hell, I didn't even have the report written yet but I was going to figure out who ran this neighborhood.

I got home that night and as it always happened, Toby called me.

He said, B*oy, I wanna' get something going in Savannah.*

Toby and I had grown a professional relationship that over about three years strengthened into an incredible friendship. I have had some close friends in my life. Friendships that took decades to form but Toby and I were friends almost immediately. We had a meeting during the formation of Toby's Operation Raging Waters in May of 2007 and I think we have talked every day since then. We see things the same way when it comes to police work. Toby doesn't spend a lot of time or energy focusing on unimportant issues. By unimportant I mean, if it is not hurting people or destroying lives then he doesn't focus on it. I'll take a second to point out, that illegal guns in the hands of criminals and drugs destroy lives. As a federal agent, Toby's job wasn't dealing with lesser crimes. He was looking at the big picture and he was a Special Agent for the Bureau of Alcohol, Tobacco, Firearms, and Explosives (ATF). A lot of people think of the ATF as a regulatory body that checks the compliance of firearm dealers, the tobacco industry, and liquor taxes. There is an arm of the ATF that does all that but the Special Agents of the ATF are probably the most proactive federal agents when it comes to combating violent crime in the United States and definitely in Savannah, Georgia.

The ATF uses innovative and aggressive techniques to get to the "Bad guys". I have been extraordinarily lucky to have been included in some of their most innovative investigations. Our brother, Lou Valoze a.k.a. Sal is considered by many to be the foremost expert in Storefront operations in the country. Storefronts were undercover ops where ATF agents pose as bad guys and attempt to purchase guns and drugs from criminals. Sal and Toby worked in several of the most successful storefront operations in ATF history. Lou details these operations in his book, *Storefront Sting: An ATF Agent's Life Undercover.*

Toby is a big picture guy. I've never seen anybody who can look at an issue, specifically crime, break it down and come up with a strategy faster than Toby. I knew the streets, I knew the problem and I knew the people. Toby knew the solution. Almost instinctively he understood what needed to be done. I told him about the gang activity I was just picking up on and he knew where to go. That night we started hunting social media. Within an hour we were back on the phone and emailing pictures back and forth of the gang we had just identified, *the Carver Village Thoroughbreds* (CVT).

We had pictures of individuals holding guns, wearing colors, and showing tattoos. We had partial names and aliases and locations we could identify in pictures. It was all there, now we just had to put the pieces together.

It was pictures like this that caught Toby and my attention. Guns, hand signs, colors (Camo), and the name CVT.

The formation of S.A.R.G.E.

The morning I returned to work after talking to Toby, I asked my Sergeant, SGT Devin Kennedy, to assign me to a beat close to Carver Heights. Beat 17 was a beat that covered multiple beats including 13 and served as backup or took calls if the beat officer was tied up on something else. It was usually covered by Corporal Gene Johnson but he was off this morning. SGT Kennedy hooked me up, he gave me 17 and I headed straight to Carver Heights. I found the houses Toby and I looked at in the pictures and plugged the addresses into our report system. I found names, looked at booking photos, and began to collect as much intelligence as I possibly could. Associates, their addresses, types of activity these guys were involved in, probation/parole status, anything I could find. I took that information and compared it to the photos we had gathered from all the pictures we found on social media and in no time, I had suspects, addresses, and a potential gang to look into. Were these the guys who terrorized the man and his elderly mother? The guys we had pulled up were a little old for that type of juvenile shit but they might be the ones the juveniles were trying to emulate. They might be the ones who were tagging everything in the neighborhood with CVT and VBS in spray paint. They might be the ones we needed to remove from this neighborhood.

In between responding to calls for service, I'd go back, look for more, call Toby and update him on all of it and I'd add it to the PowerPoint I was putting together. My blood was pumping because now I wanted to know. These guys we were identifying were into some serious shit. Drugs, Shooting, Robbery, Auto Theft, and a few other gems. All the types of shit the Feds look for when they are looking to implement crime reduction strategies. The day was winding down but I was winding up and then my phone rang. Detective Greg Capers.

He said, *Hey boy, I wanna' get something started, you got anything going on?*

I told him he couldn't have called at a better time. You might not believe it, but this is how things always kind of worked for me. The stars always aligned just when I needed them to when it came to doing real police work.

I've always considered myself lucky to have worked for some of the best supervisors. Not unlike my friendship with Toby, my relationship with Greg Capers was born the same way, out of mutual respect. Sergeant Greg Capers was my supervisor when I was a member of SCMPD's Expanded Patrol Operation (EXPO). He allowed me to work and helped me develop as a police officer. He let me make mistakes, corrected me, and showed me the correct way. Over a year we developed a trust and a friendship that continues to this day.

When I got back to SCMPD, Capers was assigned to the Savannah Area Regional Intelligence Center (SARIC) as the gun detective. It was his job to track and investigate every gun-related arrest in Metro's jurisdiction. Capers had a rocky patch when Chief Michael Berkow took over. He was demoted to Corporal and assigned to the Southside Precinct where most older cops go to retire. Thing is, Capers wasn't near ready to hang it up. I could write a whole book on Capers and EXPO…I did. That's another whole story.

Capers was in SARIC which was also where the Gang Unit was located and operated. I began to tell him about the call I had gotten the night before and how Toby was looking to put something together. I told him I was putting a Power Point together and I would have something for him soon.

Now I've got to say. I had a list of names, pictures of about 15 or more guys, and their information. When I drove around on the day shift for the next couple of days, sneaking in from other beats when I could and driving by any place I could that was recognizable from their social media, I didn't see too many of these guys. Not hanging out. I'd see one relatively often walking back and forth on McCarthy street. Going back and forth from home to the store on Stiles Avenue or Gwinnett Street. His name was Tyreek Morton, they called him "Mr. X". I just watched him, saw who he was with but never had a good reason to talk to him. He was wearing a shirt with CVT on it the first time I saw him but I was just getting started, I didn't want him to know what I was looking into just yet. Seeing him in the shirt and all the graffiti in the neighborhood let me know that this wasn't stale intel. These guys were out here.

The Feds

Since my days of working protection in the Army, I have organized any operation I was running in Microsoft PowerPoint. Pictures, arrows, bullet points, animation, you name it. It's how I keep things organized in my head. I have to see it in front of me. I did one when I was gathering intel on HVP, I did one when we were conducting Operation Raging Waters, I did one when I was gathering intel on the Dog Pound in Walthourville, I did one when I was in the cover room during Operation Statesboro Blues, I did one when we conducted Operation Invisible Fence. Now I was compiling all the information Toby and I were rapidly discovering.

The beginning of operations like this were always exciting for me. I was starting to see the picture come together and I was beginning to develop some thoughts on how we were going to go after these guys! The idea of it just got my adrenaline pumping but reality has a way of pumping the breaks on big dreams and aspirations. Being that I was the low man on the totem pole, I was back to having the shittiest, rookie cop days off. I had Wednesdays and Thursdays. So on my day off, I went to meet with Toby to discuss the grand plan. Talk about taking the wind out of the sail, working for free on an operation that I wasn't sure was even going to happen. Glamorous, no?

I walked into the Savannah Field Office of the ATF and met with my usual fanfare. This office was always one of my favorite places to be because it always meant something cool was happening. I knew everyone in the office and was excited and hopeful we'd be working together again. Lou was there with our brother, Ralf Bicknese better known to us all as Rojo because of his flowing red hair. Ralf was a former Atlanta cop who worked the Storefront in Statesboro and the middle of it transferred to the Savannah office. I can only describe Rojo in one word. Solid. I have always been honored to be able to tell people that I served with him.

Seeing Lou in the office was kind of a rare thing. He was usually traveling, helping agents across the country with their cases or neck-deep in one of his own storefront operations. Lou is the kind of guy that most cops want to be. Tall, muscular build, tattoos all over, and didn't look at all like the police. I've had several people over the years tell me about how they worked a case with Lou, no matter how small their role as they made sure to mention they worked with him. Some of them even made up stories about working with him. That's just the kind of guy Lou is. He's a guy people want to be around and if you've ever seen him work, the kind of guy you wanted to be. Almost movie star-like. Lou and I always worked well together but towards the end of our careers, when we both went through bad times, he was always there for me. I consider him a brother. Not just in the macho way that cops, soldiers, and football players call each other but in the true sense. We don't have the same blood but we are family. Toby, Lou, and Ralf are and forever will be my brothers.

Lou Valoze, Toby Taylor, and I together for the first time in several years.

Savannah had some other good agents too at the time. I knew them all pretty well and would do anything I could to help any of them any time I could and they always did the same for me. Except for the time Tom Crawford didn't get Robert Jivens III's case to the US Attorney's Office in time so he got probation in Superior Court as opposed to Federal prison time. But that's neither here nor there. I love Tom Crawford too. That office was excellent at making sure everyone helped everyone along the way.

The guy I didn't know was the new boss. Resident Agent in Charge George Belsky a.k.a. GB. Belsky was a street cop and was a U.S. Postal Inspector before joining ATF. More notable to me, GB was a West Point graduate, Class of '84. He was the quintessential West Pointer. Stocky, barrel-chested, carried himself as a leader. I'd had the privilege of serving closely with other West Point graduates in my time in the United States Army. I worked on the protective service detail of General Montgomery C. Meigs, Class of '67 who was the Commanding General of the United States Army Europe (USAREUR). General Meigs was a West Point legacy. General Meigs is the standard that I hold anyone who holds the title of Soldier to. There will never be another one like him. His great, great, great Uncle was Major General Montgomery C. Meigs the first Quartermaster General of the Union Army, class of 1836. His father, Lieutenant Colonel Montgomery C. Meigs was killed in France in WWII before General Meigs was born.

The Aide de Camp was Colonel Dan Williams, class of '85 another born leader. Colonel Williams led the invasion into Iraq as the longbow (Apache) Battalion Commander, and Major Erik Kurilla, Class of '88 replaced Colonel Williams as General Meigs Aide. Lieutenant General Kurilla now commands the XVIII Airborne Corps and had been the commander for famed units like the 82nd Airborne Division and the 75th Ranger Regiment. These three men are the personification of leadership in my eyes and George Belsky was formed from the same mold.

I cannot overstate how well I was treated in that office, especially by Belsky. I had credibility because I was with Toby, and it was backed by Lou and Ralf but GB treated me like I was one of his guys from day one. I wasn't a credentialled Task Force Agent. I was just a Patrolman that would be temporarily detailed to an operation that one of his Agents was running but I never felt like that. I could go to GB and ask for anything and he made it happen for me. I was able to succeed because he made sure we had everything needed.

Toby and I sat down and mapped out what our vision for the operation would be. It would essentially be a domestic counterinsurgency in the Carver Heights neighborhood. We would covertly insert informants to gather intelligence on criminal activity and use this human intelligence to operate a fluid strategy to rid the neighborhood of the drivers of violence and narcotics. Simultaneously, we would overtly work with city departments like the property management division (PMD) and sanitation, the neighborhood association of Carver Heights and we would consult with Crimestoppers to make sure that any tips that came in about this neighborhood would immediately be brought to our attention. Retired FBI Special Agent Demery Bishop was in charge of Crimestoppers at the time and helped us put a billboard up at the entrance of the neighborhood on Gwinnett Street which could be seen from I-16.

We knew that because Carver Heights was a proud and predominately black community we would have to be especially cognizant of the perception that we were targeting minorities. Neither Toby nor I are politicians but we both understood the importance of optics and the trust necessary to succeed in the community. We would pay a visit to the local chapter of the NAACP and meet with Chairperson Al Scott. This part of the operation would be as overt as possible. We planned on locating any possible good we could do in the community and coordinating to make sure it got done. We laid out our road map and planned to follow it until we needed to shift fire. Spoiler alert, we didn't have to shift fire, we knew it would be fluid and several months later

Chief Lovett would tell us to move into Cuyler-Brownsville. A whole new challenge but because we had the map, we had a path to follow.

We looked back at Operation Raging Waters from 2007 and saw where we could have done better and tried to include ideas we had there in this operation. The ultimate goal is to reduce violent crime by removing the people influencing its momentum.

Toby and I see eye to eye on how to police. I put it all together in a PowerPoint and after about two hours we knocked on GB's door. We showed him the road map and he only had one thing to say,

Yes, do it.

When I got back to work, I made a call to Detective Capers. I told him that I had gone and talked to Toby and that we had laid out our plan and how we were going to make it happen. Capers was all about it and wanted to see it.

That meeting was easy, We met in Capers cubicle at Headquarters in the SARIC office. Toby and Capers knew each other but they had not worked together as I had with each of them. Capers is leery of anyone from outside of our circle but like Toby vouching for me, I vouched for Toby and Capers was cool with that.

Once we had shown him the plan, and the intel we had on CVT so far Capers was all in,

Well, damn son, Capers said, *you never cease to amaze me.*

Capers was a Corporal at the time, A Corporal in a Detective's position but Greg Capers was a lot more than that. He had the ear and the trust of the Chief. Capers had already spearheaded one of the most successful proactive units in department history. He was my Sergeant on EXPO. Capers' command of EXPO got him selected as the Supervisor of the Year in 2006. So I knew Capers could make the operation happen on the department's side. Capers knew and wasn't shy about telling us that we were not going to get a lot of personnel and that he wanted our old buddy Terrance Jackson to be part of the operation. Jack was on EXPO so it was a no-brainer for me. Toby looked at me, was familiar with Jack but I nodded and that was all Toby needed. We gave Capers everything he needed and Toby told Capers the ATF was on board with the operation. I went back to patrol and they went to see the man, Chief Willie Lovett.

The Roadmap

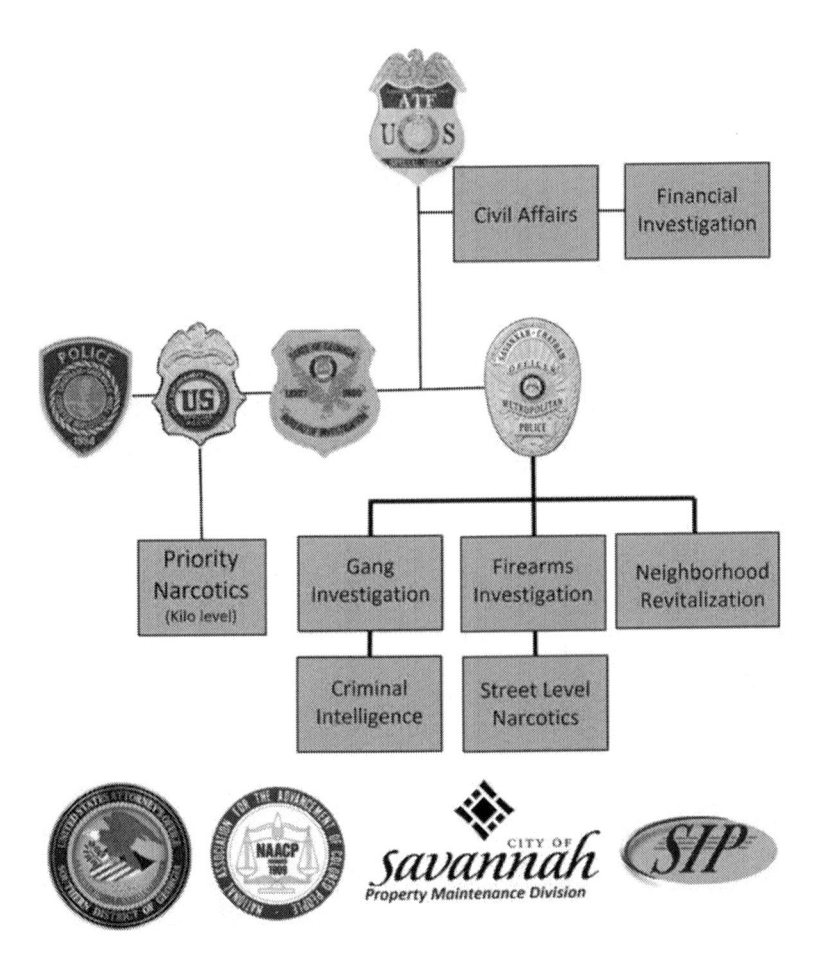

The amended "Roadmap" Toby and I laid out that morning in the ATF Office. (Note: CNT was not added until later and only to quell some political tension)

Savannah Crimestoppers stepped up and paid for this billboard at the entry of Caver Heights on Gwinnett Street. Dan Drake and the U.S. Attorney's Office gave us the cards that we passed out in the community.

It was important to have an overt presence while we were simultaneously running the covert operation.

Temporary F'n Assignment

Like everything else in my career, I didn't get promoted, no special shiny detective's badge, nothing like that. I got what I always got, a temporary assignment. That sounds like I'm complaining but believe me, I'm not. I was happy to get it. I've said this a million times, I've worked with some damn good cops and few of them got the chance to get on some of the assignments I got. I was lucky, pure and simple. lucky to know people, lucky to be in the right spot at the right time, just plain lucky. I had been given a lot of special opportunities and when I got them, I put everything I had into them. A lot of doors were opened for me and I kicked through everyone. It pulled me from my patrol assignment and dropped me in SARIC with Capers and the Gang Unit which consisted of Star Corporal Udon Carter and Star Corporal Mike Hollis. Kevin Elleby was a Savannah Police legend. I first met Elleby when I was working on Raging Waters when I was all full of piss and vinegar. Elleby had a big reputation as simply being the man. I have heard stories of when he was on Patrol that when he got out of his car, guys just got on the ground because they wanted no part of what was coming next. He was the Star Corporal in SARIC in charge of intelligence and he, Hollis, and Carter all served as a force multiplier for whatever was going on in SARIC. These guys had been around a long time and I knew all of them from years earlier. I appreciated them because they were never shy about letting me know if I was going too far or even, not far enough. They knew Savannah and were huge assets. Sergeant Larry McPhearson was the unit Sergeant at the beginning and would be keeping tabs on our progress.

For me, it was pretty easy. All I had to do was work and Toby 33could deal with the chain of command issues. I was keeping Capers up to date on everything and he could deal with any bosses and their questions.

Also, attached to SARIC was my buddy, Ronda Barefoot. Ronda had about a million responsibilities in the office but over the next two years, she was our go-to for any information on all of the guns we got. She could tell us where they came from, who was the first person to buy them, if they were stolen, where they were stolen from, and anything else we could want to know about a firearm. Ronda was a tough lady and used to give us hell if we didn't get her information on time. She kept us in line and made our jobs easier.

I make such a big deal out of the fact that it was a temporary assignment for only one reason. The temporary assignment meant I was still assigned to the patrol division, West Chatham Precinct, A Watch and I stayed on their roster which meant they had an empty slot that would not be filled or more importantly for them, replaced. So my watch mates would suffer while I was off having a blast doing all the fun shit. I've always felt bad about that. Leaving them short. This would come up a few times while I was on the assignment so I knew I had better log any and everything I was doing to make sure when the question came up of whether or not to send me back to the road, I could show them what I was doing and hope they would think I was too valuable to move.

After they met with the Chief, Toby and Capers both called me and told me that S.A.R.G.E. was going to happen. Capers told me I needed to go see Captain Kerry Thomas and show him what we had and see if he would release me to do it. That always kind of struck me funny but Capers made sure I landed in West Chatham where I could do police work. Capers knew how to play the political game within the department so I did what he said. When I got back to the precinct, I knocked on the Captain's door. I didn't know Captain Thomas but he was a real laid-back guy. I walked in and told him what I was up to and began to run the details by him. He already knew what was up. I showed him the PowerPoint and he looked at it and said he was going to let me go. He told me to let the Crime Suppression Unit (CSU) Sergeant Michelle Halford know what was going on so her unit could help and be in the loop as far as intelligence went. I told him I would but inside I had a sick little feeling. Halford didn't like me at all. To this day I'm not sure why but whatever I had done to her, she always made it clear she was not a fan. I suspect it was because she was raised over at CNT and I had done a few things to ruffle people's feathers over there during my first stint with the department. Either way, I'd keep her in the loop as much as I could because the Captain said so. I gave her a copy of the PowerPoint with the CVT intel on it on my way out. I didn't know when orders would be cut but I knew I was going.

I showed up to shift the next morning and the looks on my Sergeant's faces told me they weren't too pleased. I know now it's because they were going to be shorthanded and bodies were hard to come by but at that time I had no clue about things like that. They were also kind of ticked off because they felt I had circumvented the chain of command…well, they had me on that one but shit, I had to do what I had to do. I knew I could be more effective in this assignment than I would be riding a beat on and off.

They put me out in the county beat that morning and Star Corporal John Cain radioed to meet with him out on Fort Argyle Road. Cain was a good guy. He let me know what all the dirty looks were for but he told me to succeed and people wouldn't even remember. He was very encouraging. John Cain died a few years later after a battle with cancer. I appreciated that he looked out for me while I was on his shift.

That afternoon my temporary orders were cut, and I would report to SARIC the next morning. I was ready for this. I had a plan, guys around me I trusted, an informant who was ready to get to work, and a desire to get shit done. As I was headed to the back door of the Chatham County Annex, where the West Chatham Precinct was located, two of the SGT Halford's CSU guys were nearby and mumbled,

Anybody can put together a PowerPoint, they said.

Why didn't you? I replied and kept walking.

I scoff when I hear people talk about the thin blue line and cringe when I hear accusations about a "code of silence" where police officers cover for each other's transgressions. I started policing in 1998, The days of Serpico were long gone and the brotherhood that allegedly protected itself was long gone. The police world I know is filled with jealousy and envy. Most of the guys I know don't want to see others around them succeed. They shoot holes in any and everything other cops are doing that they aren't. I've always pulled for the other guy and if I could ever do anything I could to help them get ahead or succeed. In disgusting contradiction to what many people think, police work is one of the least loyal professions I know of. It's sad because that loyalty is needed to succeed and with the anti-police sentiment that is raging in the US today, police are getting it from both sides.

The first day I met with the guys at SARIC, Capers said we needed to present our plan to Major Barnwell. MAJ Barnwell was the Commander over Special Operations and I took it to be a check the block kind of deal. The Chief and Belsky had already blessed it so it was a go.

We went up to the war room in Headquarters and presented the PowerPoint detailing not only CVT, the members we had identified but we presented the roadmap. We explained that we expected to uncover more information as the operation progressed but that we would adapt to whatever challenges materialized.

The great thing about police work is that there is no one way of doing things and the more flexibility you build into the design of an operation the higher chance of success you will have. We had only scratched the surface of what was going on in Carver Heights and we didn't want to say we were going to target just this small neighborhood gang. We were going to embed ourselves into the neighborhood and gather the intelligence and then we were going to formulate the most effective strategy. If we had gotten in there and found that there was a human smuggling ring that's one type of investigation, drugs are a different type of investigation that require different agencies and investigators. Gun investigations are similar but have their own intricacies and another style of investigation is needed.

Toby and I knew gangs, guns, and drugs. It was our bread and butter and while we were pretty sure it would be that type of investigation, we weren't ruling anything out. We wanted to be fluid so we could create a blueprint for this type of neighborhood-based, intelligence-led counter-insurgency operation to be able to move into any neighborhood and eventually every neighborhood in the city.

Talking to brass was never my favorite thing to do because let's face it. When was the last time they worked a case or ran an investigation? That type of thing is always delegated to the lower levels, conducted, and run back up the flagpole. We requested to have Terrance Jackson assigned and didn't meet with any resistance. Though the department was short even then, one body wasn't going to tip the scales. We explained the operation and Major Barnwell listened and nodded. Like I said, I took this meeting as kind of a check the block kind of deal. Let the people in between the Chief and us know what was up and then go out and crush it. SGT McPhearson, SGT Halford, and some Lieutenants were there but ultimately, they would not affect our day-to-day. The gain here was, that we let everyone know what we were going to do and now we could stop bullshit meetings and get to work.

Snitches

So, we put this presentation together and sold it to the brass. There was no question there was a gang operating in Carver Heights and the drugs were a HUGE problem in the neighborhood. The question now was how the hell were we going to stop it? That's always the question and thankfully we usually had an answer. If you are a white boy from Connecticut it's pretty tough to know what goes on in a small neighborhood in Savannah, Georgia. Try as I might to blend in, make friends and gather intelligence…The badge, uniform, and marked police car made the drug dealers and gang members awfully suspicious of what I might be up to.

It becomes necessary to develop what is known as Human Intelligence, Informants…a.k.a. snitches. The idea is to find someone who is from an area and who has a good understanding of what goes on. An informant needs to be close enough to the people involved in criminal activity to be trusted and just far enough away not to be neck-deep in the problem. If they are too close, invariably you will have to deal with them getting mixed up in something they shouldn't be and having to deal with it, which can be a giant headache. Let's be honest, the deeper they are involved in the activities, the better they are as informants because they know the best and dirtiest information and have contact with the worst criminals.

Informants are a gigantic pain in the ass to work with. They're absolutely necessary to accomplish anything past the street level of any investigation. The first thing I told every informant I have ever worked with was that if they were ever stopped or arrested or ever caught being involved in anything they should never tell anyone that they were working as an informant. I assured them that I would help on the other end but that it is essential for things to play out naturally. Of course, this is a rule that 99 percent of them ignored in the first place. Working with informants is an art form. There are only so many classes you can take or books you can read or advice you get from other agents or investigators. There is no one way of doing it but the cardinal rule of working with informants is that you control the informant, the informant doesn't control you.

I've worked with 100 or more informants. Some had nothing of substance to offer but others provided enough information to dismantle entire gangs. The level of trust you have with an informant goes from no trust at all to, and not many cops will admit it because it is easy to get caught up in, absolute trust. I've had some very good informants and some really bad ones, I've only ever trusted one.

All that being said, without informants you are usually limited to what you can get in a subject or traffic stop. Informants are the ones that can engage with the criminals and help you get the information to develop probable cause to get a search warrant. With a warrant, you can get into where the criminal activity really goes on. If you can get inside and see where a gang member lives for example, even if it's not evidence you get an insight into who these people are and how they live. Most times though you discover a treasure trove of information on who they associate with and a lot of times, from pictures alone you can see what they are into. Pictures of gang members posing in their colors, displaying tattoos, and holding guns can be valuable evidence. Every little piece of the puzzle you can put together helps, especially in a long-term investigation. As far as intelligence gathering goes, you never know where what you find today can lead you tomorrow. Without informants, this type of intelligence and evidence is nearly impossible to obtain.

When we started in Carver Heights we had one informant. An older gentleman that I had encountered while on midnight shift before I had truly looked into all the gang stuff. This guy was doing all the things people involved in the drug game are doing. For the entirety of this book, we will call him Ben. This old fella was obviously an addict and was out scrounging for ways to pay to feed his habit. I stopped him one night after he appeared from behind a vacant house. I think he had a small crack pipe or something stupid like that. Rookie mistake to get caught with a stem but I guess if you're all fucked up it's not one of the things you think of right away. As we talked, I realized quickly that this guy wasn't a major contributor to the drug trade, and based on my training and experience I was pretty sure he wasn't out robbing or pulling triggers. The longer we talked the worse I felt for this guy. Ben was struggling with his problem and he was angry that these dope boys strung him out. He was really angry that they strung his brother out. As he told me the story about how his successful brother, who he admired had got hooked on crack and how the vultures bled him dry and fed his addiction, I could see the emotion build up. Now, this wasn't the first time I had heard a tale of woe and I was always looking for an opportunity to develop an informant. I'm not proud of it but I could see when a guy was in this condition how to turn it to my advantage.

Depending on the individual, there are different ways to motivate people to give information. With some, you hang the pending charge over their head and push them to do something they do not want to. I have found this style doesn't work very well. Most people who have experience in the criminal justice system know how much of a headache this type of thing can bring and can easily weigh if it is worth trying to work the charge off. Others are so desperate they offer up information, whether it is true or not, instantly and over-promise that they can get Pablo Escobar-level dealers even though you caught them with a gram. This case was different. I'd seen it before. Someone had suffered long and hard enough and had their own sense of worth beaten down to where they wanted to get back at the people who they felt had wronged them. I realize now after many years how predatory I had become to recognize this in other people. Though I make no apologies because I was doing these things to genuinely make the community a safer place, I still am not proud of this "ability" I had developed. I laid the suggestion that he could get these guys with very little effort on his part out on the table and, without hesitation, he agreed.

As I said, there is no one way to run an informant. I have some strong opinions about how it should be done though. An example is that many investigators who run informants don't tell them exactly how the whole thing works and what the chances of the informant's identity being turned over to the defendant are. Some investigators use informants who make it known immediately that if they are ever needed in court to testify, they simply would not come to court. I never understood making a case that I know would not hold up in court if it ever went there. Not my style. I was always very clear with anyone who gave me information on how the whole thing worked and what their exposure would be. In some cases, people who offered up the juiciest information and ones who were closest to some of the criminals I wanted to catch most would completely stop talking to me as soon as they thought there was a chance they could be found out. Ultimately, in order to make the strongest case and develop the best evidence, an informant will have to testify. So I always worked with informants, at any level like they would wind up in the witness chair. The flip side of that coin though is something that gets a little strange.

Investigators develop a level of loyalty to the people who give them information. At least, I did. If there was anything I could do to make it less likely that the informant would be identified, I did it. I always felt that no matter the reason they were giving information, they were doing something positive to help and I never betrayed that. I have always accepted that their safety was my responsibility. The risk these individuals take is immense. We live in a society now where it is more acceptable to be a murderer than it is to be a snitch. A murderer or drug dealer can walk around their community safely and even with an air of admiration following them, but a snitch? They had better be careful. No one likes a snitch. Hell, I don't even like the concept, but I needed them to be effective and I respect the contributions they have made to our communities.

One of the worst ways to run an informant is to let them lead you to what they want to give you. It can get pretty complex, for one, you need an informant to show you what you don't know. On the other hand, If you have a specific target, you need the informant to get to or at the very least around the subject you are after. Then let's mix into the equation that most of these people's motivation is entirely self-serving. They need to get out of trouble or they are feeding you their competition or they are settling an old score or whatever else. The important thing is, as an investigator, that you know the motivation and control the direction of the informant and the information. Also, you can never forget, that most of these folks are criminals and inherently dishonest. I once watched a colleague of mine get fed misinformation for months that never generated a case against anyone but it wound up costing his agency thousands of dollars in evidence funds. Like I said before, you run the informant, don't let the informant run you.

So now I had someone I knew who could buy crack in this neighborhood. I didn't need big amounts, I just needed to be able to show a Judge that crack was being sold from certain locations so I could get a warrant and discover what else we could find. I want to make one thing clear. This whole case was about gangs, guns, and violent crime. Every effort and ounce of energy that we were going to pour into this investigation was made in an attempt to disrupt and try and stop people from being robbed, shot, or killed. I don't think this is any big news flash but I feel confident saying that almost all the people who were robbing, shooting, and killing were in some way involved in the drug game. We were after guns and after more than ten years in law enforcement and three OCDETF operations, I can assure you, if you are after guns used in street crime, drugs will lead you to them.

The best, most effective informant I ever worked with became an informant because I helped his Grandmother carry her groceries up a set of stairs one day when I was on patrol. When he told me this, years after he had started giving me information, I was shocked. He said it showed him that I wasn't all about arresting people and that I cared about making the hood a better place. To this day, it is one of the greatest compliments I have ever received about my professional life.

Tang

While on patrol I had been able to identify a few spots that I was fairly certain were drug houses. All the signs were there. A lot of loitering on the steps, foot traffic, people walking up to the front door, knocking and then disappearing to the side of the house, etc. Doesn't sound too ominous but unless you're in a neighborhood where drugs are openly traded it's not the activity you see very often. Carr Avenue is a street that the only reason to use is to go to one of the houses on the street. There is nothing convenient about it, it's not a thorough way and doesn't lead anywhere. The only two reasons people go there are to get to an address or to turn and get out of sight. So, the house I looked at was down the block about halfway. Tactically, for a drug house, you could see east and west clearly and because this wasn't a thoroughfare any car on the street was suspect. I checked the address through our system and looked at old reports associated with the address to compare jail photos and identified the young man who I mostly saw sitting on the front stairs as Andrew Crowder, a.k.a. "Tang". I started collecting pictures and info like his criminal history and set my eyes on closing this shop down.

I did a similar type of research on the apartments on both sides of Styles Ave. and tried to identify the actual apartments that were involved in no good. That's not something you can get good ideas about unless you can watch for a while and Styles Avenue created a challenge as far as surveillance goes, so the next best thing was to send Ben.

I introduced Toby to Ben, they hit it off immediately. Toby and I have similar approaches to working with informants, we try to make it as painless as possible for them. We cut up quite a bit and by the time we are done dealing with the official and important stuff, they feel pretty at ease with us. Again, these are complex relationships. They have to trust you as much, if not more than you trust them. So, we jumped into the silver Chevy Malibu with the darkest tint I have ever seen. Ben felt certain there was no way anyone would be able to see him in the car and truthfully, he didn't act like he truly cared. As we drove towards Carver Heights I showed Ben a picture of Andrew Crowly. I asked if he knew this guy and Ben immediately replied:

Yeah man, that's Tang

I asked him if he knew where he lived and if he could buy drugs from him.

Shit, I deal with him all the time, he stays right there on Carr.

Well, that confirmed my suspicion. Ben said a lot of people hung out in front of his grandmother's house but he rarely let anyone in. He would sit on the stairs and serve people. When I asked the number one question I wanted to know, he told me that Tang always had a gun in arms reach.

So from an investigator's perspective, let me break this down a little. I drove to an area that is well documented as a high crime and drug area, I observed activity that was consistent with open-air drug traffic, I found an informant who gave information consistent with my observations and further gave me information that is consistent with all of my training and experience that oftentimes during drug deals, weapons are present. So, with all that information, probable cause exists to get a search warrant, right? Nope, not even close.

Now I needed Ben to back up what he had told me. I needed to know that drugs are probably being dealt from this place, the legal standard for a search warrant. I never really operated on that standard. I took it a step further, I wanted to know, beyond a reasonable doubt, that Tang was dealing drugs from his grandmother's home. Beyond a reasonable doubt as you probably already know is the legal standard that Prosecutors must prove in trial to allow a jury to convict someone of a crime. I know that seems pretty basic to most of you but believe me, there is a reason I am painstakingly explaining how and why things are done.

Since I couldn't walk up and buy drugs from these guys and we didn't have any undercover or plainclothes guys that could just walk up and buy, we had to rely on people like Ben. It is always best to get a dealer to sell directly to a plain-clothed police officer. In that case, your officer is the witness and you can charge the sale. If we used an informant, then the informant becomes the witness, and to charge the sale, they would have to appear in court which completely takes away their anonymity. The key here is to get strong and serious enough charges that the defendant will plead to the charges and not go to trial. As part of the plea deal, the informant's information is withheld. It's not exactly that simple but you get the idea.

To establish that drugs are being dealt from a certain address is a little easier, the same process but if we used an informant to buy drugs from an address and didn't charge the sale to the individual, we would have probable cause to believe that drugs were coming from that residence. That helps when there are multiple subjects dealing and when they are dealing from places that aren't their homes. The reason we go through the whole process of finding a target area, a specific location, and identifying specific people doing a specific activity is so, even though it's always changing, you have a good idea of specifically what is happening. The larger and more complex a drug investigation gets, like anything else, the more areas there are for things to go wrong.

In an investigation like the one we were doing, to rid a neighborhood of gangs, guns, and drugs, we kept it pretty simple and were well informed on who, what, when, and where things were going on. I think the Breonna Taylor incident was a result of too many moving parts and not having a good enough grip on specifically what was happening and when. As in all cases, I'm not criticizing because I was not there. Hindsight is a huge advantage when looking at incidents after they happen and have been investigated. That case appears to have been a perfect storm of what could go wrong, actually going wrong.

So, we're not even a full day into the operation and we already have an informant who can buy drugs, specifically crack cocaine from our first target. We took Ben past Tang's place and confirmed it. When we drove past, there was no one out, and not a lot going on. So we rode the neighborhood and Ben pointed out some other houses and talked about some other people doing the same kinds of things. I was pleased because a lot of the houses and locations were already on my radar. As we came up to Styles Avenue after having done a big loop, we passed the apartment buildings at Stiles and McCarthy. There was not a lot of activity there either because we were out pretty early in the morning. I pointed to the apartments on the east side of the street and ask Ben who was dealing out of this apartment. He pointed out a door and said "that's Sandman's". We talked about the exact door and he told us the Sandman was the main guy in that building and also sat with a gun on his lap when doing deals. Sounded like the exact kind of guy we wanted. We set up a time that we would meet and see if we could set up a buy from Tang and then we dropped Ben off out of sight.

I got to work immediately on identifying Sandman.

It didn't take much. When I put in the address that Ben had shown us with the apartment number, his name was all over it. Sam Burns, a.k.a. Sandman…even his alias was in the system. There were reports about drugs and fights and just about everything you would associate with your local drug dealer. This made selecting our second target a no-brainer and we already had an informant that could make it happen.

I pulled up Sandman's booking photo and recognized him as one of the guys I had seen hanging out in the parking lot on several occasions. Sandman had an impressive criminal history which included multiple felonies. Ben told us that Sandman often had a gun with him which piqued my interest because I knew, that if we could find a firearm during a search warrant we could remove him from the neighborhood for a good long time.

Recidivism in the United States is a huge problem but it is a testament to the fact that the real criminal element is a small percentage of the population. It's the same small group of people who are responsible for the crime. The state system, unfortunately, is like a revolving door. Crimes that don't carry long sentences, overcrowding in prison, and an overworked parole system. Add to it the current political philosophy of taking a soft approach on crime has allowed criminals to get out and get back in the game.

In 2007, I learned a lot about the difference between state and federal sentencing guidelines. I never spent too much time worried about how much time people would get and there is no real way of predicting it, especially if we're talking about plea deals. I always kind of figured that was for the judge anyway. I tried to make the best cases I could and never worried about that kind of thing…except…I learned there are certain guidelines, that if they are met in the federal system, carry minimum sentences. I won't get into the particulars of the guidelines because they have changed so much over the years and depend on so many different factors, but I knew if we could get certain amounts (by weight) of drugs, in particular, cocaine base or crack cocaine, we could remove some of these guys from the neighborhood for a good stretch of time.

Those guidelines have been looked at and called racist because they are said to have targeted minorities and claimed that powder cocaine is the white man's drug and crack cocaine was the black man's drug. I can assure you, as I have in the past, that drugs like cocaine in any form, heroin, hydrocodone, oxycontin, and methamphetamine do not discriminate. They eat and rot a person from the inside out. Men, women, young, old, and drugs don't care.

Toby and I looked at criminal histories and formulated our strategy on how to best deal with each individual. If they had a long and continued criminal career, they were the ones we would forward for federal prosecution and we made that case accordingly. If they were newer to the game and low-level offenders, we would make the appropriate case. If they were relatively new to the game but were driving and influencing violent crime, we had an answer for that too.

Sandman was at that time, according to the guidelines and his criminal history, an armed career criminal. If we got him with even a small amount of crack or a gun, he stood to serve a significant amount of time away from the neighborhood. One of the things you hope for in any drug investigation is that your target has a history with drugs and that they are on some sort of probation or parole for a similar offense. In many instances, especially with drug convictions, people who are convicted or plea to drug offenses often get probationary sentences that include a waiver of their fourth amendment rights. That is the right that protects against illegal search and seizure. Essentially, that means as an agreement for an individual to finish their sentence outside of a correctional facility they agree that the state/government/probation office can search their person and residence while they are on probationary status. This is a huge advantage for an investigator because the individual technically doesn't have the protections of the constitution that ordinary, law-abiding citizens have. Now, let's be clear. It's pretty fucked up when you think about a United States citizen not having constitutional protection. You have to remember they voluntarily waive that right so they can breathe fresh air. The alternative is to stay in a facility where you have no right to privacy in the first place. Also, this is after a conviction or a plea saying they were guilty. Now, if you are like me and think there is potential for someone to take advantage of this and abuse citizens' rights, you're correct. I've seen it done. I've seen overzealous narcotics investigators with time on their hands abuse situations. Find someone who is on probation, knock on their door ask for consent even though they are well aware they cannot refuse and search their residence. Illegal? No, Unethical? Not exactly, bad business? Definitely.

I'm not saying there is never a situation that would call for a knock-and-talk but I am saying that I liked to do a bit more of an investigation before I went disturbing citizens, especially ones who are out trying to change and get their lives on track. I'm a firm believer that once a person completes their sentence for whatever offense they are convicted of that they don't owe anyone, anything. It's a fresh start. A new beginning. The reason that I have changed the names of the individuals in this book is that many of them have completed their time since the operation occurred and the ones who haven't will someday be out and I don't want to slap them in the face by dragging up incidents that they have already paid their debt for. I hope they get on with their lives and have as much success as possible. You have to remember, for a police officer it's not personal, it's business. That line can easily get blurred but it's always business. If anything, I cared about several of the individuals in this case. I had a true affection for them personally but I never let that get in the way of doing my job. It's also one of the things I admired most about Toby Taylor. I don't know how to say it any other way than he gave a shit. It mattered to him. He didn't think of the suspects in our cases as numbers, he thought about them as people. I guess that is why we worked so well together.

Fourth Amendment waivers were excellent tools and for me, they helped speed up the process of my investigation. I knew that I had instant probable cause when I went for a warrant but that never stopped me from doing my investigation. I don't take labeling someone as a drug dealer or a gang member lightly. Once you are convicted of offenses that label you one or the other, it will stick with you for the rest of your life, regardless of how I feel about it. I took that responsibility seriously. So I didn't base my charges on your history, I based them on an individual's actions. Now, if you had a history of dealing drugs and I caught you dealing drugs…I had no problem going to court and calling you a drug dealer. None. I'm all for second chances but if they didn't learn the first time around, I got nothing for you. After seeing Sandman's history and the activity around his apartment the only thing left to see was if there was crack cocaine actually coming out of his apartment.

Toby and I sat down and laid out our plan. Now, we needed to make a splash right from the start, we had sold the brass on this operation and had better deliver because like with anything else in a police Department people want to see results and a few even want to see you fail. That wasn't going to happen. I knew we were right about what was going on and we were going to back up our ambitious bravado.

Buyin' dope

So, we had all the information we could get. Knew our suspects, knew the locations, had their histories and both were on probation and had 4th amendment waivers. We would now conduct controlled buys to prove crack cocaine was being sold by Tang and Sandman.

The concept of a controlled buy is simple and logical. You get an informant, search them and make sure they have no money or contraband on them, give them a recording device of some sort, preferably one that transmits so we can listen in on the transaction, and then surveil them to make sure they go to the designated location and when they return have them hand you the contraband and then search them again to make sure they didn't keep anything for themselves. After all, we are not in the business of buying drugs for addicts. Do some informants pinch some off for themselves? Yup. We do everything we can to stop it but there is no doubt it happens.

The whole logic behind the process is they go there with no dope, come back with dope after only having gone there and there is a recording and surveillance of as much of it as possible. That would lead a reasonable and prudent person to believe that the contraband came from that location. Probable cause to believe drugs are being dealt from a location. Not too complex. Very simple concept but there are huge variables and many different factors to consider for safety. Decisions to decide if you are going to charge the sale or if you are going to get a warrant all come into play and are based on the reliability of the informant, the subject's criminal history (that comes up a lot), how much time and money was spent for an investigation (shouldn't matter but hell, we have bosses too) and how far this investigation is going to go are all major considerations.

Ordinarily, I like to make two or three purchases before I go to a judge and swear out an affidavit saying that drugs are being sold by a person or from a location. It shows a pattern and that it isn't just a one-time deal. Given that Tang and Sandman were both habitual violators and I had observed enough activity to believe this is what they were up to, we decided one buy was enough. We didn't need a lot of drugs and Ben was a smoker, if he went and asked for a large quantity it would have looked wrong and few people are more paranoid than drug addicts...drug dealers are those few people. I also knew that because of the sentencing guidelines, we didn't need huge amounts of drugs to get these guys sent away for a long time.

So now the day came that we would conduct the first controlled buy. Toby and I had to get Ben, get him searched, wired up, and ready to go. We would need more people in the area to help us cover the deal so we called up all the guys from SARIC to give us a hand and even reached out to West Chatham's CSU because, after all, CPT Thomas asked me to keep SGT Halford in the loop. We positioned them to be on the outskirts of Carver Heights, far enough to be out of sight but close enough to get to us or Ben if something went wrong. The SARIC guys were all in plainclothes with unmarked vehicles and CSU was in marked units and patrol cars. I always liked to have a marked unit close by in case something went against the plan and we needed a car stopped or we needed an immediate police presence.

Elleby, Carter, and Hollis had been at this kind of game for a long time. It wasn't new to them, it wasn't exciting. They could stay away and chill out of sight with the best of them and show up when they were needed. They were good at it. The CSU guys were a lot less experienced and more excitable. I was worried they might try to get too close and make things suspicious to Tang and his crew. That said, I needed them and I was just going to have to trust them. SGT Halford had been at CNT for a long time before she got promoted. She knew the deal and rode with Toby and me. This way she knew what was going on and we could immediately have her pull her guys out if need be. I can't remember but we had one of her guys with an eye on Carr Avenue. We radioed to him what the informant was wearing and gave him the address of where Ben was going.

Like a professional, Ben left us and went directly to Tang's house, stayed for enough time to conduct a transaction, and returned to us. The whole time, Halford's guy was relaying step by step what was going on and I do mean step by step. We slowed that way down because, in the day and age of technology, we didn't want to risk someone with a police scanner listening in. Yeah, we were on a channel that was supposed to be encrypted but why risk it. All we needed was eyes on not a play-by-play.

Ben returned and as I would write in countless reports in my career handed me, "an off-white, rock-like substance that looked like crack cocaine". Crack, he handed me crack but you can't officially call it that until it has been tested by the crime lab. We did a quick field test and confirmed it was real cocaine.

Now, we got the evidence from Ben and he told us the story of walking to the house, talking to Tang and handing him $20, and Tang handing a crack rock back to him. They didn't talk much, just did the deal and that was that. It really is that simple. We sent Ben on his way. Right about that time. SGT Halford's CSU guy radioed that a car approached Tang's house, a man went to the door, was there for a second, and then got back in the car and drove off. Again, for you police-minded folks, this is activity that is consistent with narcotics dealing. It also occurred to me, that if we could find out drugs were purchased from Tang by another individual it was an even more solid search warrant.

SGT Halford told her guys to wait until the vehicle was away from the area and to see if they could find a legitimate reason to stop the car other than seeing them conduct what they believed was a drug deal. Of course, we didn't want them to mention being anywhere near Tang's house because they would go right back and tell him we were watching. They waited until the car came back out onto Styles Ave. and drove towards Cloverdale. I don't remember exactly what they stopped the car for but it was something like a seatbelt or equipment violation. There were two men in the car and after a short conversation they gave up the small amount of crack and marijuana they had purchased. Neither man would say where the drugs came from and really, we didn't need them to. This was just one more piece to show that 1225 Carr Ave. was involved in the drug business.

Right about this time is when things got interesting for the Savannah Area Regional Gun Enforcement Task Force. In early October, when we all met with the Majors and briefed everyone on the operation they promised us at least one person to help. By early November, we still didn't have that person. That is until Toby went to see Major Tolbert with some flowers. That Toby boy had some serious style to him. He could have bitched, moaned, emailed, etc., and made a stink that the PD wasn't holding their end of the deal up but no, not Toby. He walked into the Patrol Commander's Office, with flowers and said "Ma'am, Terrance Jackson was supposed to be detailed to us and he still hasn't got his orders." A phone call was made, orders were cut and my EXPO brother was at work with us the next day. Just in time too because the paperwork was about to start piling up and we needed help before it bogged us all down.

There is no easy way to describe Terrance Jackson, he is one of a kind. Suffice it to say he was all street cop. Jack had worked the hardest neighborhoods in Savannah and come out with the respect of the guys on the street. He was hard but he was fair. He didn't sweat the small shit and he was not shy about breaking his foot off in someone's ass if it called for it. Truth be told, we needed Jack for two simple reasons. The first was we needed someone we could trust and I will trust Jack until the day I die. The second was there was a strong possibility that Capers would be getting (Re)promoted to Sergeant in the next round of promotions and we were trying to make sure Jack had the resume he needed to get the Gun Detective slot that Capers would be vacating shortly. Jack's experience was all on the street, in patrol, and Crime Suppression. He didn't have any experience in investigations so S.A.R.G.E. would give him that and put him in SARIC where the gun detective already worked.

Grimy you say? Lining someone up for a job before it is even posted? I guess that depends on where you sit in the situation. I was a Patrolman. Had lost any seniority I had when I left the department three years ago. I came back and was even referred to as "Recruit Grogan" when I was detailed to this assignment at Capers and Toby's request. In the grand scheme of having juice, I was on the lowest possible rung…if you looked at it on paper. Terrance Jackson had ground his daily routine out in Tatemville, all over Central Precinct while training countless numbers of police recruits. He did this after humping a ruck and riding in the back of a Bradley armored vehicle in the Gulf war as a member of the mighty 24th Infantry Division. Also, just to point out, this move put him in the best position to get the job, it didn't guarantee him anything. Jack's work always spoke for itself. He and I butt heads like family but we always cross the finish line together. S.A.R.G.E. got stronger the second Jack showed up for work.

We set up and executed a controlled buy from Sandman a couple of days later. Ben was again just like a professional. Got in, got out, and got it done.

After the controlled buys, we had everything we needed for search warrants on Tang and Sandman's places. We needed to make a splash and show the brass we could do what we said we were going to do. Even though we tried to emphasize this would be a long-term investigation. It never hurts to be able to show progress at any level. Also, guns and drugs would go a long way to being able to show the U.S. Attorney's Office that we were on the right track.

I typed out the affidavits detailing all the information we had gathered for each address, the people involved, their criminal history, and that firearms had been seen at both. I applied for a "No-knock" clause for the warrant. 100% candor. I always applied for a "No-knock" when I was serving drug warrants. Two huge factors need to be considered when applying for these clauses. One, is the target violent or known to have firearms? Guns and drugs go hand in hand. It is a proven fact, that most drug dealers protect their drugs with guns. The second factor is what are the chances that evidence can be destroyed if entry is delayed into the dwelling? I mean, why waste the time or expend the energy to do a search warrant if you are just going to allow the target to flush his cocaine down a toilet?

I've never taken a "No-Knock" lightly but if you do enough search warrants can easily become a "check the block" proposition. This is not a critique of others or an apology for the way I conducted business but rather a plea to Investigators to keep the importance of the overall safety of everyone, good guys and bad guys alike at the forefront when applying for warrants. If there is a tactical, lesser use of force available, use it. That said, In 2011, I used "No-Knocks" on almost every warrant because we were going after drugs but more importantly we were going after guns.

So at this point, we were using city PEPI (Purchase Evidence Purchase Information) funds to purchase the evidence, so all the warrants would go through Georgia Recorders or Superior Court as opposed to

Federal court. Honestly, it was a hell of a lot less red tape and it was a far more efficient process. We could move a lot quicker. So we did. I got warrants signed and now we needed to figure out the best way to execute them.

To execute a "No-Knock", you need manpower. A lot of it. We could have piled the guys from SARIC, West Chatham CSU, and maybe patrol and gone and hit the door, but when you're executing a warrant like this, why not use the guys who train for it? SCMPD had a S.W.A.T. (Special Weapons And Tactics) team. They were a part-time unit where Officers worked their regular assignments, trained monthly for S.W.A.T., and responded to call-outs as they came in. These guys may have been part-time but they were serious and very good at what they did. I contacted Sergeant Rob Gavin, who was a S.W.A.T. Team leader, and told him we had two warrants we needed to serve and we needed S.W.A.T. He was all too happy to oblige us. S.W.A.T. guys love getting call-outs, it's why they do all the extras to be part of that team. I want to point out I'm not a real "Hooah, Hooah" guy. I never had any interest in S.W.A.T. because I had already been in Baghdad and kicked enough doors to last a lifetime. When I was at M.A.C.E. we essentially were the S.W.A.T. team and we served almost all our own warrants by dynamic entry. I have a true appreciation for what they do and I was thankful that they were willing to go through the doors on my behalf.

Along with S.W.A.T., we would need K-9. During my first three months back at Metro, I don't think I had any contact or called for K-9. When I was getting prepped for these two search warrants I called SGT Greg Ernst, The Metro K-9 Commander. Ernie, as he is affectionately known, is a cop's cop. I once heard Ernie referred to as the guy, "If I was shot or murdered in Savannah, I would want Ernie leading the team to get the motherfucker who did it."

I called Ernie and the conversation was quick.

"Sarge, it's Grogan, I have a detail up and running and I need K-9 support", I said

"When and where do you need us, brother?" was his response.

There was no question about what unit, who was doing what, who authorized the use of K-9…none of that. I had earned Ernie's respect years ago and he trusted me. That is the kind of trust that drove me to make sure I knew exactly what I was doing. The kind of trust that guys like Sergeant Armando Tamargo, Sergeant Greg Capers, SGT George Gundich, ATF Resident Agent in Charge George Belsky, and

Special Agent Toby Taylor placed in me drove me to be better at my job. I took it seriously, it meant the world to me and it held me to a standard. I am forever grateful for their trust. He told me Corporal Eric Dukarski would be there and I asked if they had any explosive or gun dogs. Ernie told me he would contact the Chatham County Sheriff's K-9 and get one of their guys there too. I worked with CCSO's K-9 when I was at MACE. They were top-notch also.

With warrants signed, S.W.A.T. and K-9 support all lined up, all we had to do was pick a time and date. Drug dealing is a 24/7 operation so knowing when the best times to hit a place really depends on the level of the operation. Since the only intel we had on Tang's operation was from a very low-level addict that knew some things, but not who supplied Tang, when he re-upped, or how much he bought at a time. Also, given that we were pretty easily able to identify what was going on by a simple drive-by and controlled by, the level of sophistication was minimal. A search warrant is good for ten days. If you don't execute the warrant in those ten days then the information that led to your probable cause is considered "Stale". This prevents investigators from holding on too long and allowing situations to change too drastically. I've always thought that was a very good check or balance to make investigators stay sharp and know exactly what is going on in the given situation. We weren't going to wait. Drug dealers have crazy hours and we knew from Ben, that Tang didn't like to be disturbed in the morning time. So, I thought we might disturb him a little.

I've executed warrants on locations where people I know are drug dealers at places that I know they deal drugs from and still come up with nothing. We were starting a long-term operation so coming up with nothing on the first warrant would have been bad, real bad. I always got a little nervous, even though I know I had done my due diligence and could prove to anyone that drugs were being dealt from Tang's house but, hitting a door, causing damage, using this much manpower, and coming up empty? That's fucking embarrassing. Toby and I are friends but he was still a federal agent and I was just a temporarily assigned patrolman, I didn't want to look bad. More than that, I was just coming back to the department, got pulled off my watch to form a special detail, Capers stuck his neck out and told the Chief I was the guy to do it, I called in S.W.A.T. and K-9, and the other guys from SARIC. They were all watching closely to see what I was going to do. A lot was riding on this one.

We briefed at the Chatham County Annex. I put together a PowerPoint presentation that briefed all the people involved on our target, the location, and what each unit would be responsible for. I had aerial photographs of Tang's house and the Carr Ave. I mapped the route from the Annex to the target and I used a series of "moving dots" to make sure everyone knew where they were expected to be and how they were expected to get there. I tried to think of everything everyone could need to know. You can never cover every angle but I sure as hell tried. This was quite a show of force we had assembled and I needed it to go smooth.

A flashbang in bed

So after giving the brief, S.W.A.T. gave their brief and made sure each member of their team knew their role. These guys had it down to a science. Each move was accounted for. We wrapped up the brief, asked if there were any more questions and when there were none, we went. It was a decent drive from the annex to 1225 Carr Ave and my stomach was a little sick. The toothpaste was out of the tube and there was no getting it back in. We rolled and like a well-oiled machine we were on the target in minutes. There was nothing I could do. S.W.A.T. hit the building and it was on. S.W.A.T. Officers went to the sides of the house and the breacher and entry team went to the door. BOOM!!!!!!

The flashbang went off and the breacher hit the door. All I could do was wait for the "all clear" signal to come on the radio. It was seemingly forever before the S.W.A.T. Team Leader came to the door and waved me to the entrance. Members of S.W.A.T. were piling out of the house as I approached and it kind of seemed like they were in a hurry to get out. I got to the door and asked if he was in there,

Somewhere, the Team Leader responded.

I thought that was a strange answer until I broke the threshold of the front door, missing floorboards, and piles upon piles of rubbish like a hoarder had lived here. There was no running water, there was feces on the floor and the floor joists bent when you walked on them. When you first enter the house there was a front porch. Past the porch, there was a hallway that led to a kitchen that had no floorboards. A quarter of the way down the hall to the left was a bedroom which is where I saw Tang for the first time. He was on his stomach in handcuffs on the only clear space on the floor next to a mountain of clothes. I'm not exaggerating when I tell you, this pile of clothes was four feet high. The window next to the bed was smashed from where the flashbang was thrown through it. It landed on the bed next to Tang and served as his alarm clock. I can't even imagine what it is like to lay next to a concussion grenade when it detonates but I could see Tang was pretty dazed.

There was Crack all over the dresser in this room, marijuana, scales and packaging material, a box for a Sig Sauer 9mm, and some ammo. The box was in a gun case, like the ones people use to go to the range. It had a cleaning kit, ammo, extra magazines, and things like that. I've been on a lot of search warrants but this case was a little out of the ordinary for the hood. I don't know too many gangsters that have a kit to go to the range. So, we ran the serial number that was on the gun box.

I wanted to clear the entire house of personnel so the K-9s could come in and do their sweep. Dukarski and Nado would search for drugs and Jay Livie and Aldo would search for guns. We all got out and let them do their thing.

I took Tang out to one of our vehicles and interviewed him. It was much like all the interviews I have ever conducted in this type of situation. He admitted to selling drugs but said someone had left that gun case there. He seemed particularly nervous about it. Of course, everyone on the street knows, you don't want to catch a gun charge because federal time is real. If you get it, you do it. No parole and they don't send you to a local prison. You could wind up anywhere. We asked about the box but the fact that there was no gun and he deflected saying the guy who left the case, took the gun which could be a plausible explanation.

I interviewed Tang for a little while and Toby called the property maintenance department (PMD). We had no idea how bad the house Tang was living in but it was an atrocity that a human being would be living in these conditions. The structure itself was falling in, there was barely a floor and there was no running water. I don't even want to know the list of health hazards this man was living in.

Dukarski came out with Nado and said there was Crack all over the place. He walked me through it and pointed it out so we could collect it all. Livie was sweeping still and Aldo kept going back to the four-foot pile of clothes. Aldo had alerted on areas where we knew bullets were and he was stuck on the pile of clothes. We lifted, sorted, and moved all these nasty clothes and didn't find anything.

We had the K-9s step out and we started to collect the evidence. The serial number on the gun box came back through the national crime and information center (NCIC) as stolen out of the Atlanta area. It would turn out later that this gun was stolen from the son of an ATF Agent. Small world huh?

So, we got our bad guy, got plenty of crack to charge him with but were only sniffing around a gun. The PMD S.W.A.T. team as we called them, showed up and immediately condemned the house. I want you to think about that for a minute. A house in your neighborhood is known as a place where drugs are being dealt. It gets hit by a S.W.A.T. team and the local drug dealer gets hauled off to jail. Then, the city comes in right behind and boards up the house to prevent any further habitation of the building. That's a strong statement if you ask me. The partnership between us and PMD became a strong one.

We had been on-scene for about an hour. The S.W.A.T. team had cleared up and we were bagging the last evidence and I was at my car when I heard Toby yell "KEV-IN!". I knew by the tone in his voice something big had happened. Toby never calls me Kevin. I went to the door and looked into the bedroom. Jay Livie was standing there, Aldo was on the bed and the pile of clothes had been moved to where I could see a Sig Sauer 9mm with a silver slide and black frame laying on the floor. Aldo had kept coming back to the pile, people kept searching but no one had gotten to the very bottom of the pile. Aldo wouldn't come off it and Livie knew his dog didn't act like that unless there was a reason. He could have pulled Aldo out, we could have missed it, but we didn't. Like I've said, getting the drugs are great. We didn't come up empty. The guy we said would be there with drugs…was there with drugs but we also said he had a gun, and he did. Getting guns out of the hands of drug dealers will always be our mission.

Crack, marijuana, scales money, and a stolen gun. This was exactly what we needed from our first search warrant. This wasn't a drug raid. It was a raid to get rid of the guys hurting the neighborhood.

Specificity

So, now we had one success under our belt but we had a long way to go. Capers was pleased which told me everyone above him was pleased because if they weren't, he'd have let me know. GB liked that we were off to a good start so he decided that he would come to the next one.

We had another search warrant to get ready for and hope that we would have the same kind of success. I went back to my drawing board and put the PowerPoint on Sandman together "with circles and arrows and a paragraph on the back of each one explaining what each one was". Again, I used aerial photos and moving dots to make sure everyone knew where to go. I had a picture of the front of the building and a big arrow pointing to Sandman's door. I didn't want to leave a lot to the imagination.

This target had a few challenges the other did not. This was an apartment building. Sandman's apartment was flanked on both sides by other apartments and one above. These were all tactical considerations and S.W.A.T. would cover all those bases but my name was on the affidavit. I wanted to consider any and everything that could go wrong, God forbid something went wrong, I'd be the first one answering for it.

We did some light surveillance the day leading up to this warrant to see if we could catch a glimpse of who might be in the surrounding apartments. I was especially worried if there were any children. The problem was that once you hit about 10 in the morning, there was a ton of movement on the corner at Styles Avenue and McCarthy Street, so any police parked or lurking in the area was easily noticeable and we didn't want to draw any attention to the fact that we were paying attention to Sandman's apartment. Remember, we knew we were going to blow that corner up, the drug dealers didn't…yet.

Search warrants and police presence was not new to the Carver Heights area. It was a high crime area so everyone, good and bad was used to seeing the police. They had no idea how much of a police presence they were going to get in the coming months.

The next briefing we would give would be at the Downtown Precinct. It was close and a direct shot to Sandman's apartment. I gave my briefing and S.W.A.T. laid out their directives. It was decided that I would ride in the front passenger seat of the lead vehicle and when we were on target, I would exit and point exactly to Sandman's door so there was no mistake. As I said, I had put a picture of the front of the building with a big red arrow pointing to the door but why risk it? We were going to hit the right door.

It was as hell of a thing to watch this convoy of vehicles, headed to the next target. Again, we were hitting it in the morning hoping we would get to Sandman before he was awake. We pulled off Styles Avenue into the small parking lot right in front of the apartment building and I jumped out and pointed. The S.W.A.T. team swiftly and fluidly breached the door. There wasn't a long delay this time. The team Leader came right out,

He's in there on the couch, he said.

Well, good start, the guy I said would be there was there. I looked around as the S.W.A.T. team started to exit and unlike Tang's, the floor was solid beneath our feet. I gave a quick look at the living room area and didn't see anything worthy of note. It's not always just laying out in the open, but I started to look around. Tables, drawers, refrigerator, freezer, cereal boxes…all the common hiding places. There was a little scratch (marijuana leaves) but nothing worth even collecting. I peeked my head in the bedroom and had a similar finding. I went back into the living room and saw what looked like the grip of a pistol underneath the blanket on the couch Sandman had been sleeping on. He was now on the floor in handcuffs. I began to smile, now we were getting somewhere. I moved the blanket and found a pistol….an air pistol that is. Not what I was hoping for and the lack of obvious drugs was starting to concern me. My phone rang while I was walking around and Dukarski and Nado were doing their sweep. I was walking, talking and was a little nervous because now I was talking to the big boss. I was trying to give him a SITREP while I was thinking. I told him we had Sandman but that all I was seeing so far was misdemeanor type things. Now, this wasn't what I wanted to be reporting and I was wandering in the apartment now. I was in the bedroom as I relayed the misdemeanor news when Duke tapped me.

He was pointing to Nado who had his nose pointed directly at a DVD case that had crack rocks all cut and spaced for sales.

Is crack a misdemeanor now? Duke asked with his typical shit-eating grin.

I was happy to report we now had what we needed. This would be enough crack to remove Sandman from the neighborhood for a long time. Not because it was a lot of crack but because of his criminal history. GB was pleased. Two search warrants, two successes, and two federal defendants

Crack, scale, money, and the air pistol we seized from Sandman

The DVD case with the "misdemeanor" crack laid out on it.

As we collected the evidence, S.W.A.T. K-9 and the guys from SARIC all cleared. There were a lot of people gathering around inquiring about what was going on. Tang's house was less than 200 yards from Sandman's but it was around the corner and tucked away. This was right on the main drag, Styles Avenue and people saw all the commotion. Only two days after we hit and boarded up Tang's house so I was pretty sure at this point the criminal element was taking notice.

Two young men appeared a little more interested than the rest. Toby and I, being ambassadors for progress decided to introduce ourselves. These two guys were more interested in what was happening at Sandman's than I think we were. Joseph James and Stephon Pickens were all too curious why the "feds" were interested in Sandman. We talked a little bit and told them we were doing our best to clean up the neighborhood. Joseph, who was known as "Bookman" said he had done some time in federal prison and wanted no part of it. We of course pointed out the obvious, if you are not involved in drugs or gangs, the feds would have very little interest. Neither Bookman nor Big Hoss liked that answer.

At this point, we knew we had the neighborhood's attention. At the least, the "Top" of the neighborhood. Carver Village had unofficially been divided into the Top and Bottom. The Top was the eastern border around Styles Avenue and the bottom was closer to the western border and the park that was located on Carroll Street.

I did a little homework on Big Hoss and Bookman. I had seen Bookman on McCarthy Street while I was still on the watch but I had never noticed Big Hoss. Turns out, he lived right across the street on McCarthy from Bookman. I'd do some digging and see what we could come up with on the two of them. As I said, they seemed a little too interested and concerned about what was happening. Bad idea to draw our attention to them but sometimes that is all it took.

Chatham County Sheriff's Office Jason Livie and K-9 Cpl. Aldo. Aldo retired in 2003.

SGT Erik Dukarski and K-9 Nado. This dog made me feel dumb but they always made our jobs easier.

Example of the photograph I had attached to the affidavit for Sandman's apartment.

We arrested Sandman in late November, he was indicted by a federal Grand Jury in February. A couple of weeks later, I was on the witness stand in federal court answering a motion to suppress by Sandman's defense attorney, Julie Wade.

Ms. Wade was a former Assistant United States Attorney and a very good lawyer. She cited my affidavit, and spelled out that I had not specifically named Sandman's door, which I had written as "the second door from the right of the building". The problem was there were two doors that were second from the right as you faced the building. One downstairs and one upstairs. I did not specifically point out that Sandman's door was on the first floor.

It was a valid argument. I should have written it in the affidavit and I didn't. So here I was answering for it on the stand. Ms. Wade framed it in the light that I did not know specifically what door we were going to hit and made the inference that because I had not purchased the crack from the location I didn't have first-hand knowledge of which door it was. That was her job, to kill my credibility and to represent her client to the best of her ability. I have to admit, she did that.

It's for all those reasons that I did my surveillance, debriefed my informant, and used pictures to illustrate exactly where we were going to execute the warrant. When I went to the Judge to get the warrant signed and explained my probable cause, I brought the same picture I had used in the briefing. A picture of the front of the building with a big red arrow pointing to Sandman's door, on the first floor. It's also the reason I rode in the front seat of the S.W.A.T. vehicle so I could jump out and point to the door, on the first floor where Sandman had been selling crack.

My testimony satisfied Judge Smith that I knew, before executing the warrant I knew exactly which door was Sandman's. He denied the motion to suppress.

I will never forget when he turned to me, while still on the stand and said, "I'm sure Agent Grogan will remember to write more specifically in his next warrant". He was correct. I would never forget.

Police are not perfect but they do their job to the best of their ability. Everyone makes mistakes but just because mistakes get made doesn't mean there is some sort of corruption or dishonesty going on. That is important to remember.

I appreciated Ms. Wade for doing her job. There is a misconception that law enforcement and defense attorneys don't get along with each other. I learned a lot about how to make better cases from some of the best defense attorneys in Savannah. Mike Schiavone, James Byrne,

Don Montgomery, Steve Sheer, Steve Beauvais, and others showed me that the relationship is anything but adversarial. Schiavone is a throwback to the days when a handshake meant something. Mike's concern was not whether or not his client was guilty or not guilty, he focused on the law and believes that every citizen has the right to a quality defense. He wants to make sure his client's rights are protected and that if there is a doubt, he raises it. I have nothing but respect for an attorney who is working to protect the constitution. I admire it. Ms. Wade was doing her job, her duty and it made me better at doing mine.

By a fucking school? Nah dawg

We met with Ben and told him how the search warrants went. He told us that no one was talking too much about snitching but everyone in the neighborhood seemed to be concerned about the "Feds" being around. Ben kind of chuckled,

You know who y'all should get? That Motherfucker Softy...dealing to parents picking up the kids from school.

Toby and I were caught off guard. Obviously, we wanted to know everything we could about that. On the north side of Carver Heights, there was a school, the Oglethorpe Academy, It was just north of Gwinnett Street on Hastings Avenue. Right at the corner of Hastings and Hadley Street, there was a house. Or a run-down shack. Toby and I knew the house because we spent a lot of our mornings on the other end of Hadley Street parked behind two houses that were boarded up and tagged with CVT and VBS. I may not have mentioned this before but VBS stood for "Villa Boy Soldiers". We would sit behind these two houses and this is where we met the notorious Gangsta Dog. Gangsta Dog was a strung-out-looking Jack Russell Terrier who protected his little patch of turf from the crackheads that would ride through his lane. He was a no-bullshit dog and had all the mannerisms of his real-life human gangster counterparts. Gangsters live and die in the streets. About a year after S.A.R.G.E. pulled out of Carver Village I returned one morning and saw the man who lived in the house where Gangsta Dog used to chill. I inquired as to where GD was and the owner replied,

Petey? Man, he got dognapped. I guarantee, he didn't go without a fight. TIP Petey.

In the afternoon, cars would line up to pick up students 50 yards from the front door of the school. Kenny "Softy" Johnson was selling crack. The line of cars formed in front of his door and he would serve whoever walked up to his house. That shit was going to stop.

It took a little investigation to figure out who he was because Ben only knew him as Softy but with the address and some other information, we got booking photos and Ben picked him out. A little more digging and we found out he had an active arrest warrant out for him. That was all I needed. We would just go and hit the house and serve the warrant.

I set up a briefing and we intended to simply serve the arrest warrant, lock this guy up and keep him from selling crack so close to a school. We invited PMD to come with us in the hopes that this shack was in rough enough shape that they would board it up and keep anyone else from setting up shop. It was a simple operation and it went smooth.

We got there, approached the house and Softy was right there. We took him into custody in the front room where there was a little more crack. So, in addition to the warrant he already had, we charged him with possession. Now let me make this clear. This was an old man, not some huge contributor to the drug trade but he was dealing crack across the street from where kids went to school and played. If we were really trying to clean up a neighborhood, we couldn't ignore this. So off he went.

This building at 106 Hadley Street was barely standing, they were running electricity from the building next door by an extension cord and there was no water. Unfit for human habitation. PMD came in and boarded it up. Another strong message to the streets.

About a week later we got a call from an old buddy, Bobby Banks with the Georgia Bureau of Investigation (GBI). Bobby was a good guy, a former Savannah cop who was assigned to CNT and saw through their shit pretty early. He joined GBI and kept doing drug work. He was aware that we were looking at Carver Heights and had just picked off four kilos of cocaine coming to an address on Allen Street.

That's a hell of a lot of dope. If we weren't already sure, this confirmed that we were in the right neighborhood. Bobby said he would keep us posted as he followed up on this case.

Having GBI attached to the case would be helpful for us. They could do all the high-end drug stuff while we tried to clean out the street-level stuff and keep getting guns. To get a case to qualify for the Organized Crime Drug Enforcement Task Force (OCDETF) funding and prosecution, you have to have a Federal and local agency with a nexus to narcotics. ATF is not a drug enforcement agency so we needed an agency that's primary focus was drugs. GBI was our state-level narcotics task force. Toby was a GBI Agent before getting on with ATF so it was a good fit and neither Toby, nor I were big fans of the Chatham County Counter-Narcotics team (CNT). I had bad run-ins with them earlier in my career and never had a good feeling about the way they did business. Toby was not a fan at all after his last major OCDETF case in Savannah when, on their own, CNT backed out and decided to help DEA cover a wiretap case. Now it turned out just fine because Savannah's Tactical Response and Prevention (TRAP) team stepped up under the leadership of Sergeant Lavon Oglesby. SGT O and his guys took me under his wing and showed me the ropes of narcotics investigation during Operation Raging Waters and I remember what he taught me to this day.

I will never forget standing in SARIC when Chief Lovett came walking in. Toby and I were standing there talking about GBI and also talking about getting started on the OCDETF proposal. I could write another book on the benefits of working a case under the auspices of OCDETF but suffice it to say, it made it a lot easier for everyone to fund an operation with OCDETF money. The Chief said hello and Toby started to brief him a little on what was going on. They began talking about the case going OCDETF and Toby told the Chief about the kilos that GBI had intercepted. He said we would need to decide who we wanted to use for the narcotics nexus. Chief looked at Toby,

I don't want CNT anywhere near this, GBI works fine. He said.

That answered any question Toby had on the subject. A funny story followed that. Once we were deeper into the operation, Toby had a conversation about this with his old boss. Roy Harris was the Director at CNT when Operation Ruffian was going on. We started in October but it wasn't until February that we brought the operation to the OCDETF Committee and it was approved for funding. CNT didn't give a shit about what we were doing until we got OCDETF money. CNT had always been DEA's "Do boys". If DEA needed something, CNT would always do it. If CNT needed something, DEA might help them but only if it benefitted DEA. So, for example, when the DEA ran a wiretap case and used CNTs' facilities and personnel, DEA would cover CNT's salary and overtime for that operation. That's a big benefit to a county drug task force's budget. Similarly, OCDETF money could be used to pay overtime for local or state personnel who were working cases jointly with federal agencies. Because DEA's mandate was strictly narcotics, at least in the Southern District of Georgia, DEA kind of felt like OCDETF funds were theirs. They were not big fans when the ATF, whose purview wasn't narcotics specifically got OCDETF funding for operations like Raging Waters, and Statesboro Blues, and the FBI got OCDETF funds for Operation Invisible Fence. OCDETF funds were used to purchase all kinds of evidence in those operations especially, drugs and guns.

When we attended the OCDETF meeting, it was known then that GBI would be our narcotics nexus for Operation Ruffian. Again, that was a decision that was made by Toby and Chief Lovett. DEA opposed OCDETF funding going to this operation and to be truthful I forget what their official opposition was but I remember thinking they were mad because they felt like we were dipping into their stash and we were leaving their little brother out of it. Not a professional response to an initiative that was designed solely to reduce violent crime. I fucking hate politics. We got the funding anyway despite their objection.

Toby and Roy Harris met shortly after. Toby had worked for Mr. Harris while they were both at GBI. Toby sat down and Mr. Harris reasonably wanted to know why CNT was not used as the nexus seeing as though most of CNTs personnel were from SCMPD.

"Is it because of Kevin Grogan?" Harris asked.

Now let me explain to you how absurd of a question that is. ATF Special Agent Toby Taylor was the case agent on Operation Ruffian. Kevin Grogan, that's me, was a patrolman, who was temporarily assigned to SARIC to support the operation after having only been back at the department for three months. The Director of the multiple-agency, county-funded counter-narcotics team was asking a federal agent if a patrolman was the reason they were left out of the operation (ergo, out of the funding that would have paid salary and overtime because CNT was never really too interested in violent crime).

Toby explained that the decision had been made by him with Chief Lovett's input. This was business, not personal. Neither Toby nor Chief Lovett had confidence that CNT would be a benefit to this operation so Toby went with the agency that already was helping us, nothing more than that. When Harris left CNT and the next director came in, Toby met with them also…They asked the same question. Someone at CNT thought Kevin Grogan had some serious fucking clout.

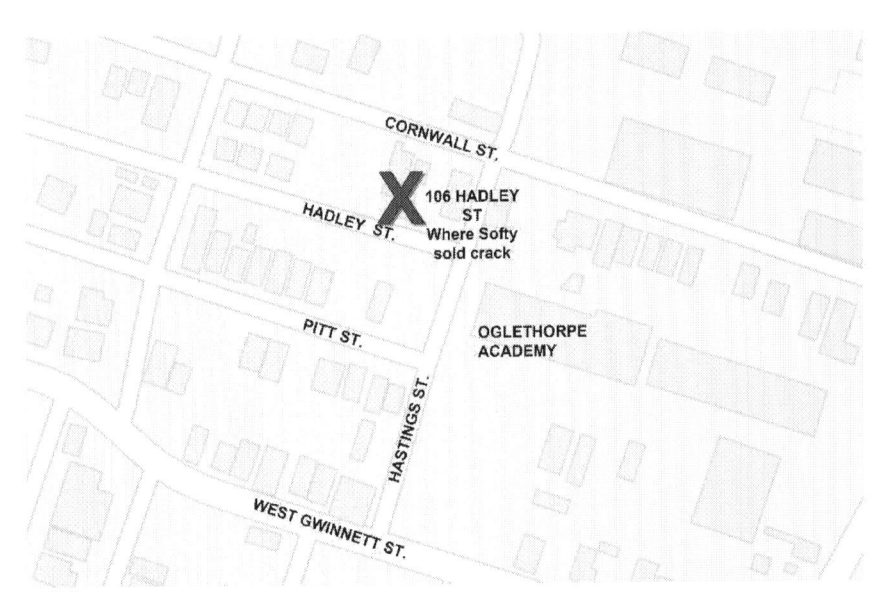

This is a map of the northern part of Carver Heights. The red "X" is where "Softy" was selling crack cocaine. The map gives you an idea of how close it was to the Oglethorpe Academy, where grade school children were learning and playing.

106 Hadley St. and 1225 Carr Ave. after the PMD S.W.A.T. team boarded them up. A well-orchestrated team that helped clean up a neighborhood.

I hate to say I told you so, but...

There is another apartment building across the street from Sandman's building. Ricky McFadden a.k.a. "Chunk" was a large man who lived on the second floor and was selling drugs. Chunk wasn't a guy who had a violent history and we didn't suspect he was driving violence in Carver Heights, but we couldn't allow him to keep feeding poison to the neighborhood if we hoped to slow the activity at this intersection. So, as you would in a garden if you're pulling weeds, you have to pull all of them. If you leave one, in a week, your garden is full of weeds again.

We did two controlled buys from Chunk's apartment. During the first buy from Chunk's apartment, Chunk himself didn't come to the door, a younger man served Ben. We wanted to shut the activity down and, in this case, we were less focused on the who and concentrated on the where. Because we were only making buys to get probable cause for warrants as opposed to charging the sale to an individual, who was far less important. We needed drugs to stop coming out of this apartment on this corner in this neighborhood. We did the second buy and Chunk did the deal.

So, we had served two very public warrants and made somewhat of a show out of both of them. Feds, S.W.A.T., K-9, and Property Maintenance, and still, right across the street these guys were comfortable selling drugs. I think the reason is that this neighborhood was used to seeing police come and go. They would hit and then move on. There hadn't been a sustained presence in any one particular neighborhood since 2007 and that was on the eastside. So these guys probably figured once the police got one or two, they would be gone. Wrong, we were vested and we weren't going to let anything slide.

We did the same thing we had done on the other cases, briefed with moving dots and we hit the door early one morning. The apartment was full of people. A one-bedroom apartment with 6 or 7 people living there including young children. The young man who had made the first sale was there and when we identified him, we found out he had a probation warrant.

There were very few drugs in the house, a misdemeanor amount of marijuana, not what we were after but enough to arrest McFadden. He was going to bond out that afternoon and go about his way but we were trying to send him a message. Toby and I sat with Chunk in Toby's car and we talked. We told him to look around and told him we knew why he was dealing drugs. He wasn't trying to shine or get rich, he was doing it out of necessity. We understood but obviously could not condone it. Chunk wasn't the kind of guy we were going after other than the fact that he had an extensive criminal record. Our goal with Chunk was to get him to stop dealing drugs in Carver Heights. We explained to him who and what we were trying to do and he understood. Genuinely you could tell Chunk got what we were saying. I learned early in my career not to lecture people you were going to charge. Toby and I simply told him that when he bonded out the dealing needed to stop completely. Chunk got the point. He bonded out and within a matter of days moved out of that apartment. As far as I was concerned, we got our message across. It wasn't about handing out huge prison sentences and solving the issue with incarceration. It was about getting the destructive activity to cease.

Now I wish there was a happy ending to this story. We told Chunk to stop dealing drugs. A federal agent and police officer sat down and asked as nicely as possible for Ricky McFadden to stop selling drugs in the community. We didn't limit that to Carver heights, we asked him to stop. A few months later, our favorite informant told us the Chunk was selling crack over in West Savannah, just a few blocks from where we executed the search warrant. We kind of took that as a giant "fuck you". The street is all about credibility. If you say something you better be able to back it up. If you don't, or worse can't, back it up you need to shut up, or eventually, someone will pull your card. In this game, police are no different than the criminals they deal with. We needed to have the credibility that when we told you something you knew it was true. If I told you were going to jail, you were. If we asked you to stop doing what you were doing and you continue to do it, it means you think I'm soft. It's the old; don't mistake kindness for weakness. Some people only learn one way. Chunk was going to see, Toby and I were men of our word.

Even though it was a few blocks away and technically out of Carver Heights, we would make the time to deliver our message to Chunk. Our informant was a certified and reliable informant who had made hundreds of cases for us before he began purchasing quantities of crack cocaine from Chunk. When the time came to serve all our arrest warrants, we grabbed Chunk up and charged him with distribution of cocaine base (crack). He was sentenced to 160 months in federal prison, which is more than 13 years. At his sentencing, Chunk stood before the Judge,

Do you mean to tell me, you had a federal agent ask you to stop selling drugs and you continued?

All I can say is we tried it the nice way. He ignored it and we aren't soft…I hate to say I told you so, but I told you so.

Everything we touched was going our way. Would we have liked to get kilos of cocaine out of McFadden's apartment? Sure, but he wasn't that level of dealer and we didn't expect it. We were being thorough and wanted to surgically remove the trouble.

We bumped into Bookman a few times on McCarthy Street and it wasn't long before he stopped coming around. He moved deeper into the neighborhood. He got the message that this corner was indicted and it didn't pay to be around there.

I had done a little homework on Big Hoss also. He was always hanging out in his front yard but after the Sandman search warrant, I wanted to know more about him. Turns out he had a warrant for probation violation that was active. So, one Friday afternoon, I got Capers out of the office, and me, Jack and the Ol' Sarge went for a ride.

Big Hoss was posted on the front lawn, so we got out to say hello. Toby and I had been around enough where most of the fellas hanging out weren't too surprised by us getting out and talking but when the three of us got out, you could see there was a different feel. Big Hoss backed up behind the car that was parked out front and I slowly walked down the driver's side, Capers stayed at the trunk and Jack moved swiftly down the passenger side. Big Hoss was focused on me so I approached very non-confrontationally. His eyes were on me but Jack was on him in no time. Jack was an old man even then, but he was still quick. He had his hands on Big Hoss and I closed the distance on my end.

Big Hoss was tense,

Why y'all up on me? he protested.

I told him he had a warrant for a probation violation.

Man, that's bullshit, I done checked with my P.O.! again protesting.

True or not, I confirmed the warrant before we went looking for him. So he was under arrest and would have to sort it out with his probation officer. While being placed in handcuffs he was stiff, not resisting but not exactly complying. I told him to chill out and relax but he was fidgeting and making it difficult to get the cuffs on. Only for a few seconds but something was up and when Jack went into his pocket, a search incident to arrest, we found out why. Big Hoss had a big hunk of crack in the watch pocket of his jeans. Now he had a bigger problem than just probation and my suspicions about him being involved with Sandman were confirmed. That's just how it goes sometimes. Go for one thing and find something else.

So, Capers drove and let us do all the work. Typical. It wasn't a lot of work and Capers always had something up his sleeve. He told me to come to see him when we got back to work after the weekend. I met him at his desk in the SARIC office and he handed me a case file. Like I've said Capers was the gun detective and dealt with any and everything the department had to do with guns. He had a case from a pawn shop where an individual had pawned a gun. Nothing too alarming about that. Just because it involved a gun didn't necessarily make it a violent crime and pawning a gun in and of itself, isn't even a crime. The issue here was the person pawning the gun was a convicted felon. He left his name, address, and even his fingerprint on the paperwork, on purpose. The address was smack dab in the middle of Carver Heights. So now, we had a chance to introduce ourselves to this young man and see where it went.

I looked at the name, Anthony Charlton Moore, a.k.a. Charley. Nothing about it jumped out at me. I looked at his history and, while he had a lot of arrests in the past and some of them felonies, there was nothing to indicate this was a guy we needed off the streets. He had forgeries and some drugs. The thing is, you can't judge a person, especially a criminal, by what is on the paper in front of you. I have met some really bad guys that had very little in their criminal history and some really good guys that had rap sheets that would make Pablo Escobar blush. The thing about our society is many people think that all criminals are just bad. It's not the case, the more people I have dealt with I've learned people sometimes do some pretty bad shit when they are in bad situations but it doesn't make them bad people. Keep that in mind, please.

So, Charley had an address on one of the streets in the middle of the neighborhood. I already knew this guy had no luck in life, I mean, he pawns a gun using an address that just so happens to occur at the time that the federal "Gun Police" start an operation in his crime-infested neighborhood. Any other time, this one may have slipped through the cracks and he would have gotten his $350.00 and been on his way, strike one. I looked at the file, assessed it, and drove over to the address.

Charley's picture was on the top sheet and as I drove past, guess who walked out of the front door. Actually at a location that is listed on his paperwork, bad luck...strike two. I was all by myself in an unmarked vehicle when I passed him. I didn't want to draw any attention to what was about to happen, especially not in the neighborhood. I needed to talk to this guy but I didn't have a warrant yet to arrest him. I would need a justified reason to stop him, to make contact. I got on the radio and called for a marked unit to make a stop. My boy Godfrey was not far away. I told him to wait till Charley was out of the neighborhood and then see what he could do. Godfrey found a reason and when Charley was out of the neighborhood, he got stopped.

I wasn't far behind and I approached as Godfrey was getting Charley out of the car, turns out he had some weed in the car with him...strike three. That's a bad day. So now, instead of saying no, I don't want to talk to you, Charley didn't have a choice except to come with me and listen to what I had to say. I let Charley ride with me, we didn't tow his car and arranged for it to meet him at headquarters. I called Toby and he would meet us there too.

There wasn't a lot to say in this case. I didn't need Charley to admit to anything, we had all the proof we needed and because this was already on its way to being an OCDETF case, the US Attorney's Office would already be willing to prosecute this case under Project Ceasefire. Charley's criminal history didn't make him the ideal target but the fact this offense was right in the area we were paying all this attention to meant he would go to federal prison unless we had a reason to not let it go that way.

Most people who have experience in the court/prison system know the drill. They get charged, they do some time, but they get paroled or probated sentences all the time. It's a revolving door. They also know, that the federal system is a lot different. If you go to federal prison, you will serve at least 85 percent of your sentence and there is no parole. Once you're out, you are on federal supervised release and that is a hell of a lot tougher than state probation or parole. Not that anyone would ever want to go to prison but *no one* wanted to go to federal prison.

Toby and I had a long talk with Charley and made sure he understood the situation he was in. He knew the game, turns out he knew the players too. Like I said, on paper Charley wasn't much of a criminal but when we tapped into his experience and knowledge base, he was a treasure chest of information.

Now, potential informants had fooled us before. They talk a great game and have very little follow-through. We could let Charley walk and hold the charges over his head. Then once he was free of headquarters, we might never see him again. We could take warrants and have to go looking for him and the chances of him walking out the door of the only address we had for him twice? Doubtful. Toby and I had done this many times and we had a pretty good feel for people. Trust me when I tell you, we succeeded with people far more often than we failed.

Charley would go on to provide us with information and make buys for us that would separate this case from any we had worked before. Charley was a gigantic pain in the ass but if being an informant was his job, this motherfucker was good.

That's what you signed up for...

While Toby and I plotted and tried to gather intel. Jack was just getting the lay of the land. I rode him into the neighborhood and showed him some of the spots we had identified. Now, Jack had a familiarity with Carver Heights from 2006 and our time on EXPO but he was a Central Precinct guy. Jackson knew the streets, he understood the feel of it and as we drove around, I explained the more community-oriented side of our aggressive police strategy. It was not like EXPO where we called in the cavalry and swarmed, this approach was far more methodical and even surgical. We would find the tumors and cut them out and leave as much surrounding tissue undamaged as we could. Jack got it but you will never take the street cop out of Terrance Jackson. We turned off Gwinnett Street and headed towards Hadley.

There was a young man posted at the top of the lane and when he saw us, made an immediate turn to come in our direction. We were in an unmarked Ford Taurus, with a black guy driving and a white boy riding, in the hood that spells one of two things, a drug deal or…The Police. By turning towards us and closing the distance we would have to give ourselves away and jump right out on him or we would have to keep going and turn around which would give him distance and a better chance of getting rid of anything he had on him.

I don't think it's a well-known fact but people run from the police all the time. They do so for a lot of reasons. They run because they get scared. They run because they are not sure if they have warrants. They run because they have something on them that they need to get rid of before the police discover it on them and sometimes, they run just to fuck with the police.

Just to be clear, this kid hadn't done anything wrong. Nothing illegal. He was just in a place where we know, statistically and from experience, that drugs are being dealt. His sudden turn when seeing the police drew our attention to him and as we drove past him his concentrated stare at a fixed point directly in front of him told me this dude didn't want anything to do with us. I know what you're thinking, we are in an unmarked car and driving down the street, maybe he didn't know we were the police. Possible but unlikely. Songs have been written, Young Jeezy famously exclaimed,

"Ford Taurus pull up, everybody run. White boys jump out, pointin' with their guns. Ford Taurus leave everybody came back, hope them boyz didn't find my sack".

In the early 2000s and into 2010, a Ford Taurus was almost as recognizable as a marked Patrol car and with the combination of Jack and me in the front seat, if he didn't know we were the police, he should have his hood card revoked.

Jack saw the same thing I saw and before I could say anything, he sped up, veered hard right at the intersection, and turned around. The young man in question, who was now looking back at us over his shoulder then broke into a full run. So, being the inquisitive guys we were, we pulled alongside him as he ran. He ran past a lane, he ran past a fence, he crossed Gwinnett Street and ran past a few houses. His mistake? He ran in a straight line. He kept running, we kept driving. We slowed at the stop sign to cross Gwinnett Street and caught right back up to him because there was no traffic. He was getting tired and we were getting excited. Jack had been at this game a long time and this kid had not. He was running out of gas and decided to turn into a driveway. Jack slowed just enough for me to jump out and I was on him in seconds. He got halfway down a very short driveway and threw something that didn't even make it the other half of the very short driveway. This poor kid was gassed.

I put cuffs on him and noticed he had CVT tattooed on his wrist. Jack went and retrieved whatever he had thrown. It was a bag of marijuana, well, several small bags of marijuana all bagged up for sale. Not a lot of weed but it was consistent with exactly what we thought he was doing when we first saw him.

A stop or incident like this is commonplace in police work. Experienced officers recognize behaviors that ordinary people don't see. One of my biggest frustrations is when I see segmented videos get posted on the news or social media and people react,

He wasn't doing anything, why are they fucking with him? they say.

To an untrained eye, yeah, I might agree. They might not see him doing anything but trained professionals with years of experience and training see more. Like a person with scoliosis, or flat feet walking across the food court in the mall. I would look at them and not notice a thing. A trained orthopedic surgeon can look at their posture, the gait of their step, the way they hold their head, and see a host of symptoms that are nearly invisible to the untrained eye. I've seen cops stop people for seemingly no reason and I wondered but when I talked with them and they explained what they saw from their angle, it made perfect sense.

Hell, I initiated stops before I could fully articulate why I was making the stop. I'm not saying I stopped them for no reason, simply that I couldn't put everything that I was seeing into words immediately. Sometimes you have to react before the situation changes because, when you're dealing with dangerous people, it can go bad, fast. I am thankful that when the situations I put myself in turned bad, I was able to get the upper hand fast enough to avoid any of us being seriously hurt. It doesn't always turn out that way.

Shoulda', woulda', coulda' doesn't do a lot of good in life and death situations. In the streets, if you hesitate, the consequences are eternal. Reacting to things too quickly has a negative side to it also. Sometimes being aggressive can put you in situations where the aggression is too much for the outcome. I can't tell you how many times I've grabbed an individual and thrown them on the ground or against a wall because they made an unexpected movement towards a pocket or their waistband, only to have it be they were adjusting their pants or reaching for a breath mint. Anyone could have looked at that and been critical,

He didn't have anything on him, or *You put him on the ground for no reason.*

Well, none of it is for no reason. There have been times in those same circumstances where that unexpected movement was a grab for a gun or pulling up their pants so they could adjust and get a position of advantage to swing at me. Those are situations where, for $18.43 an hour, I wasn't willing to lose.

That's what you signed up for.

Nah dawg, not this guy. I'm going home at the end of the day and if I have anything to do with it, so are you. Well, sometimes you're going to jail but hey, that's the game.

Does it happen? Over-zealous police exerting power over individuals for no reason at all? Yes, it does. Acceptable? No, absolutely not, but do we live in a country where police exert that type of force consistently and operate with impunity? Hell no. Hell, in this day and age police can't get away with spitting on a sidewalk much less an actual abuse of power.

The misperception of police misconduct has become crippling to law enforcement in America.

Clearing out what we can

So, around this time, our superstar informant who had worked with Toby and me for years returned to Savannah after a tour of Georgia's correctional facilities. Working with this guy was like clockwork. He always called when we needed something to break, Charley was looking like he might be able to get the job done but this guy? He knew everyone, everywhere and he was just out of prison so no one was looking at him cross-eyed about getting back in business.

He made a few sales cases on some of the remaining dealers in the neighborhood. Guys that seemed to be ignoring that we were kicking in doors and wanted to pick up the business left behind by Tang, Sandman, and Big Hoss. Over the next month, we developed sales cases on a neighborhood rapper, took care of Chunk once and for all, and got a guy who decided to ignore what was going on around him at Styles and McCarthy. They were all sales cases of crack from guys who had significant histories.

The rapper, we'll just call him Screwface, when it came time to lock people up on sales warrants, I caught Screwface living in a house in midtown Savannah. There was a stolen gun underneath the mattress and because he was a convicted felon, he let the woman he was living with, who was in the bed with him when we served the arrest warrant take the rap for the pistol to try and get less time when it came to sentencing. That always sickened me. A guy who was "bout that life", "Ain't no snitch" and acted like there is some sort of honor in the hood lifestyle, letting a woman take charge for him instead of accepting responsibility. Screwface wound up getting 48 months for his drug dealing but dodged a bullet, like a coward allowing this woman to take his charge. I regret charging her but she stepped up and claimed the gun was hers. It was stolen so she was charged with theft by receiving stolen property. She was a little surprised but took the charge "like a man," unlike her man.

While we were making sales cases with our old CI, we kept Charlie busy too. We also watched what was happening with the guys we had identified as being in CVT.

The arrest Jack made on our CVT member who didn't know to change direction in a foot chase just confirmed to me that CVT was operating in this neighborhood and there was a definite tie to drugs. Sandman and Tang didn't have all the CVT shit tattooed on them, and they didn't show up in the pictures on social media, so they were only linked by the area. There was also no way to show any tie between this kid and his weed and any of the guys we had already arrested. I wanted to know more about these CVT guys and it wasn't long before they got my attention.

Bobby Franks a.k.a. Big Bobby and Alonzo Merriman a.k.a. Zo got arrested about a week later. They were two of the CVT guys we had identified from social media. They were prominent in several of the photos of the gang standing and holding their fingers in the shape of a C and a V. There was a shooting at a downtown nightclub and these two were arrested in possession of firearms. Big Bobby had a sawed-off shotgun and Zo had a .380. As soon as their names showed up on the blotter, I looked into it as much as I could. The detectives working the case didn't have much of a back story and the victims didn't appear to be members of any rival gang, at least that we knew about.

In 2010, there was little accurate gang intelligence in Savannah. We didn't have a lot of information and we sure as hell didn't track it for long because after all, using the word "gang" was strictly forbidden. We'll talk more about that later.

I dug a little deeper and found out that these two were both at a murder scene a few months earlier and both of them had guns then too! Why the fuck were they still on the streets? Well, that's how the system goes. Neither one of them had a serious criminal history yet so they got first offender diversion treatment and probation after spending a little time in jail.

Also, one of three brothers we identified from t-shirts and social media got picked up on the eastside in a stolen car with a .380 handgun on him. So CVT was operating all over Savannah, but they were not doing anything in the neighborhood. At least not enough to draw our attention. From the pictures and from what I was seeing on the street, there was no question there were 30 to 40 guys who were identifying themselves as CVT, and from the types of things they were involved in, it was definitely what the law considers criminal street gang activity.

During January, I caught parade duty. I had to stand along the parade route on MLK by Popeye's near Kayton Homes. As I stood there a group of guys came walking toward me. Guys I had never met in person but I can't say I didn't know them. I had been studying their faces and knew each by name as they walked behind a man who was clearly the leader.

His name was Charles Sanders, they called him "Chaos". I had seen him in pictures holding guns in his camouflage holding his hand to make the letters "CV". I knew he was on probation, I knew his home of record and I knew him on sight, without ever having talked to him.

Mr. Sanders, what's good? I asked him as he got close.

He looked at me inquisitively, not sure how to react.

Chaos, right? I said and held up my hand with a "CV".

The group's eyes got large and they started looking around in disbelief.

I asked, *Y'all know who I am?* as they began to walk away.

Nah, Chaos said as he walked away.

You will soon enough, I said.

It was just a head game, to get their minds wondering who and what was watching them. I wondered where it would go but only time would tell.

I don't like to get into statutes and laws etc., because I don't think it is all that entertaining to read about but to make this point, people need to understand the law and how it is applied. I have always felt that charging someone with a crime is a huge deal. I mean, I literally arrested more than a thousand people in my career and there are guys who have made thousands of more arrests than I have. Like any other job, it becomes somewhat of a routine and the more you do it, the less each one, unless they stand out, really registers in your mind. As you all know, an arrest, even a small or seemingly meaningless incident can alter the course of a person's life forever. In the digital age, once an FBI number is attached to your name and information, it can follow you for the rest of your life. Anytime someone runs your information, depending on their clearance level, this arrest will show from the moment you are booked on.

I always felt that it was a great responsibility to make certain, even before accusations, much less formal charges were made in certain cases. For example, if I was going to accuse someone of being a drug dealer, I would know for certain that they dealt drugs.

Gang member is a hell of a label to put on someone. Can you imagine going for a job interview, when they looked at your background and saw you had been charged with violations of the criminal street gang and terrorism act? That would raise a few red flags, so it is not something I took lightly when I looked at these guys. The way the law is written makes it pretty easy to group someone in with a gang because, let's face it, you don't have to be an actual member to influence or participate in the activity.

Georgia law defines a "criminal street gang" as, and I am paraphrasing, any organization, association, or group of three or more persons associated in fact, whether formal or informal, which engages in criminal gang activity (murder, violent crimes, kidnapping, drug dealings, weapons violations, major thefts, etc.). The existence of such organization, association, or group of individuals associated in fact may be established by the evidence of a common name or common identifying signs, symbols, tattoos, graffiti, attire, or other distinguishing characteristics, including, but not limited to, common activities, customs, or behaviors.

Now lots of "groups", as one Savannah Police Chief liked to call them, can associate formally or informally and have a name and symbols but what sets them apart and what made me focus on them was always their activity. HVP/HVC, LVK, CBV, VBS, CVT...all acronyms for their neighborhoods. I always found it a little odd that people would tattoo the name or abbreviation of their neighborhood on themselves just because they were proud of where they were from. So, I always figured there was a little more to it.

I worked a case in Walthourville, Georgia. A sleepy little town that was overrun with drugs and violence by a gang that called themselves the Dog Pound Gangstas or DPG. I got the chance to interview several of them and they all, to a man, denied that DPG was a gang. I would ask general questions and they would always deflect and come up with some other explanation for a tattoo or t-shirt. I got to know each one of them. I looked at the charges I brought against them, who they were with and even looked at past arrests and saw who they were arrested with or who they were with when the others got arrested. It almost always involved drugs or guns. When I got to know the individuals, I would observe they had DPG painted on a car, a tattoo, a picture, or t-shirt on a wall in their house, or something like that.

One day I got to interview one of them as a result of a search warrant I had gotten to take pictures of his tattoos. He was in jail and had no real expectation of privacy but to be thorough to make sure I could use each of their tattoos as evidence for a case I was building, I wanted to make sure I could show a judge before I charged anyone that there was probable cause to believe that this gang existed. I found it interesting that before I served the warrant, I would ask each of them to consent to let me take the pictures, and again, to a man, they denied their consent. Imagine how pissed they were when I handed them the warrant saying they head to let me take the pictures. This guy however was really amicable. He wouldn't consent to let me take the pictures but when I handed him the warrant he was like, damn, and was cool about it. He had "Dog pound" tattooed across his chest.

What's that all about? I asked him.

Man, you really want to know what that is? He replied.

Yeah man, bad enough where I went through all the steps to get a search warrant, I said.

When we were kids, we all had pits and hung out and let them play. We just all loved dogs, he lied.

I said, R*eally? How old were you when you did all that?*

Like 13-14, he said grinning like it was a good memory.

So, let me get this straight, you were 14 just hanging out because you all loved dogs and chillin', right?

Yeah man, there's nothin' more to it than that. He smirked.

So, where'd you get the tat done? I asked

He replied, *Shit, I got that down the road* (Prison).

I looked him dead in the eye and made one statement.

Bruh, so you're hanging out with a bunch of dudes because you all like dogs when you are 14, then at least 7 years later, you get locked up, come to jail, get sent off to prison and you get your teenage group tattooed on your chest.

I didn't have to keep talking, I just looked at him. He dropped his head for a second and looked right back at me with a smile,

We can talk about something else?

That told me everything I needed to know. These guys would deny everything even when faced with cold hard facts. This guy was respectful though, he was done lying and chose just to change the subject. I could respect that. From that point on though, I had no problem calling him a gang member.

After looking at all these guys we had identified as CVT, the pictures they had all over social media, and the types of crimes they were now all getting arrested for, I also had no problem calling them gang members. Though, I do have to stress it was important to me to know if they were members or just associates and whether or not their association was formal or just a loose association. I didn't want kids who were on the periphery to get dragged down into this hole with guys who clearly didn't give a fuck.

Things were going well. We had put a dent in one part of the neighborhood as far as drugs were concerned and the word was getting around. Our search warrants were successful and now we were making purchases of cocaine from individuals that were what we considered to be mid-level dealers. Along with that, we were now starting to see some progress on some of our smaller community projects. We were getting graffiti removed from the streets and the parks. We were also taking steps to get some of the trash that was being dumped picked up.

I was keeping a timeline and taking photographs of just about everything we had done up until this point. I also added all the information about the CVT members and the drug activity. It's just how I organized and tracked what we were doing. I have to admit, it also came in handy if one of the higher-ups came and wanted to know what I was doing, I could hand them this packet and, in a few seconds, all they would say is

Yeah, keep doing that.

Capers gave me a call and wanted to meet with Toby and me. We all met up and he told us that the Chief wanted us to present the operation at a meeting he was having the next day. The meeting was set up by a local pastor, Dr. Ricky Temple. The way I understood it was that

Dr. Temple was trying to find a way to help with the crime in Savannah, which had 21 murders in 2010. Dr. Temple saw the solution as being more than just a police operation. He wanted to get leaders together to discuss the problems and the solutions. Chief Lovett thought enough of what we were doing to put us up as an example of what the department was going to start doing. Chief Lovett, Mayor Otis Johnson, District Attorney Larry Chisholm, and a few others attended to discuss some options. The Superintendent of Schools was going to attend also but had a scheduling conflict. I was encouraged to see this collection of people because these were the decision-makers and it showed a willingness to look at a problem from several different angles.

Toby and I presented S.A.R.G.E. as an example of an alternative enforcement strategy. Some very proactive policing combined with a community-based approach to include several departments of the city. Mayor Johnson watched with a grin and nodded while Toby, a born presenter, outlined the road map we had come up with those months ago. Mayor Johnson was a no-nonsense kind of mayor. He was the mayor in 2006 when Chief Lovett formed EXPO and went after the bad guys hard. Mayor Johnson was behind us all the way both then and now.

It's one thing to have different law enforcement agencies cooperating but to have the city behind us too was a huge confidence boost. It's easier to do your job when you know the chain of command agrees with what you are doing and has your back. Just a note, that's exactly what is wrong in law enforcement today. The police are willing to do their jobs but the city, county, state, and federal governments are too lost in the politics to support the men and women who are laying it on the line in the streets. Without that support, we will continue to see rises in the crime rates.

We were on a mission to succeed. Toby and I always were. We understood the importance of political support but we didn't worry about it, we were as non-political as it gets. We looked at things simply, to keep the good people safe from the bad people. The fact that we were not getting any political opposition just made it easier to do our jobs. It is amazing what happens when governmental units work together for a community and even more amazing when no one cares who gets the credit for success. Unfortunately, that is a rarity. All too often the good of the community gives way to the need for votes and to justify budgets and other obstacles to progress.

We also knew how to play the game. We knew to be seen and we would go to neighborhood association meetings to try and make contacts in the community. Chief Lovett was such a fan of what we were doing he had us attend a neighborhood association meeting where John Barrow, the district's Congressman attended to give our presentation. These meetings were important for optics but we didn't get a lot out of them, to be honest. The meetings were usually attended by an older crowd and they weren't the ones out in the streets. They were more worried about quality of life issues, like when people took their trash cans back in off the street and bushes covering the neighborhood signs.

The President of the Carver Heights neighborhood association was a lady who had at one time been a state senator, Ms. Dorothy Pelote. She cared a lot about this neighborhood but she wasn't, as you can imagine, plugged into what was going on in the street. Reverend Chester Ellis however, had a better feel for what was going on and it was clear he was fed up with the activity. Chester let us know when we were on the right track and helped with any community projects we put together. We had a couple of days where we did cleanups on Stokes Street and one on Endley Street. Not exactly a police function, but how can you claim to care about a neighborhood and drive by empty lots that are filled with trash? We justified the time we spent cleaning by saying the dumping was illegal and therefore should get our attention but again, City Hall and our Chief knew what we were doing so there was no need to justify anything. Just do it. That's how shit gets done.

Getting sloppy, and that's dangerous...

Toby and I had explained to Charley that it was guns that we were after. We wanted to get the guys who were selling drugs that had guns and Charley responded,

That's all of 'em, he said.

Even so, we treated every controlled buy or deal as if the person we were dealing with was armed. Not only because of their history but more because of the nature of the business. If you are dealing drugs and you are not armed the chances of other dealers robbing you of your stuff is pretty high. That's just the game. I mean Sandman had a BB gun just to look like he was armed, to deter people. Some faulty logic but it gives you some insight into that world.

Charley took us around and showed us a few spots that we already knew about and a couple of new ones. We prioritized and chose one we knew, at least to the extent that we could know, was armed.

The house was on Porter Street and it was a guy who already had weapons charges. Kevin Saunders a.k.a. K-Rock did not have an incredibly long history but a decently violent one. He was also on probation and had a fourth amendment waiver. Let's face it, if he's dealing drugs and has a firearm while doing it, this is the guy we want to remove from the neighborhood. This was also our first chance to see if Charley could do the things he said he could do.

I did all the investigative things I needed to do before we sent Charley in to buy. Because Charley was more of a criminal that was involved in dealing and not just using, we would have to buy larger quantities to make it look realistic. If Charley walked in looking for a $20 rock from K-Rock, he would have thought Charley was smoking and not trusted him. A reasonable amount for low-level dealers is about a quarter ounce or a "Quarter" which should cost around $250.00 depending on the buyer's relationship with the dealer.

We didn't want to spend a lot of money but it was more important to find out if Charley was at the level we thought he was at in the drug game. We needed someone who could do more than buy smoker-level drugs because eventually, we would be looking to get guns. If Charley couldn't buy a "Quarter", then no one was going to sell him a gun. No one knows how unreliable a smoker is better than a dealer.

We set up the buy, went through the process and Charley returned with a quarter ounce of crack. He said it was definitely K-Rock and that he was alone in the house. Charley said he didn't see a gun out in the open during the deal.

In the same fashion, we had been doing everything, I got a warrant signed and a couple of days later, we served it. We briefed at the Annex again and had a convoy that stretched a good long way. I had Jack put his eyes on the target to make sure we had a real-time account of people coming and going. When the briefing was done, we rolled down Chatham Parkway onto Telfair and got to the railroad tracks. CSX was at the intersection and there was a train approaching at about 7 miles per hour. I mean this thing looked like it was going in slow motion but still, it was a fucking train. I was in the lead vehicle and jumped out to talk to one of the guys. Just to give you an idea, if we had kept going the train would have split our convoy in half and it was long enough that I could not see the last car of the train. So, with my badge displayed and all the command presence I could muster,

Stop the train! I yelled,

No, he replied.

Ok!!!! I folded.

I mean, I don't know shit about trains but I know enough about physics to know it would take some doing to stop all that weight even if it wasn't moving very fast. I went back to my vehicle, dejected, and looked at Mike Hollis who was in the car behind me. He shrugged his shoulders,

Yeah, there's no real class on how to handle that. He said.

So we sat with our thumbs in our asses while the train passed at an alarmingly slow pace. It seemed like forever but it might have slowed us up for about five minutes, then we were back on our way. When we got to the house, I jumped out and went straight to the front yard so I could get out of S.W.A.T.'s way. I hit the ground and looked towards the front door and saw something that made my heart skip a beat. There was a camera facing the front of the house so if anyone was monitoring they could see everything that was coming.

Why is this a concern? Well tactically, you want the element of surprise so the bad guys have no time to react and if they see you coming, they have, even if only a few seconds, 1: Time to get ready and grab weapons or 2: Time to destroy evidence. I was sick to my stomach because I had missed this camera when I drove past to get intel on the house and potentially put the S.W.A.T. guys at a higher risk.

When they hit the door I was on pins and needles.

Thankfully, K-Rock had only chosen option 2. When he saw them coming, he went straight to the bathroom and started to flush. When he was taken into custody the toilet bowl was swirling and only one little bag of cocaine was still floating in the bowl. Who knows how much went down the drain? Given the choice, I'm glad he chose this one. We found drugs and a gun. That's what we were there for.

In the grand scheme, it was a successful warrant but it stayed with me from that day on. I got sloppy and even though no one was hurt, they could have been and it would have been my fault. That camera was in plain view, not hidden or obstructed. I missed it, I missed it because I was careless and sloppy and I would never let that happen again.

On a positive note, Charley was one for one. His info was on time so there was hope for bigger and better things to come. The other side of it was that for whatever reason and I don't remember why, two CNT Agents came along on this warrant. I'm sure it was some kind of "heal the relationship" type deal. I remember the sick feeling in my gut thinking they had now seen my fuck-up of missing the camera and that we only got a little bit of dope. To be honest, that's the one I would have loved to pull 90 kilos out of but…fuck it. We got a gun and that was one less gun that was in the drug business that could be used to hurt people. I'll chalk that up as a win every time.

Note, that we wouldn't see or hear from CNT again for months.

It's funny to me that in retrospect, of all the people, good or bad, and all the agencies I had worked with and near, I have such a negative feeling towards CNT. I've known a lot of very good cops who were assigned there over the years but, as a whole, I have nothing good to say about CNT.

I guess holding grudges like bad judges is something I didn't know about myself. I'm also a horrible chauvinist. I didn't realize that until after I had very unconsciously omitted almost every female officer I have ever worked with and the positive influences they have had on my career from my first book. I wrote it and gave shout-outs to all the great police officers I have worked with and without a thought, left all the women out.

Now, to be clear, I have served in combat with women in the Army. I have served on some pretty tough streets in Savannah with female officers and I have never doubted their abilities to do the same things I did on the street, at least not because they were female. A good cop is a good cop. I've learned a ton from several women I have had the privilege of serving with. I'm just old-fashioned in my thinking when it comes to gender roles. I've seen soldiers and police injured and wounded and I was affected differently when the officer or soldier was a woman. They stepped up and did the same job I did, many of them did it better than me. I always judge or measure other officers on merit, never their gender but the fact that I had almost to a person, omitted the women I worked with, showed me something about myself that I wasn't fully aware of. The greatest omission I made was that of Corporal Jenessa Stalter. J taught me as much or more as anyone I worked with and I love and respect her for it. This is my formal and public apology to her for not writing that in the first book. Much Love J.

So when this book comes out, I know it will ring a few bells and cause many people to call me racist or whatever for the thoughts and opinions that I express. This is a free one, if you want to call me a chauvinist or sexist, you got it. Guilty, I confess. When I think about it consciously, I have all the respect in the world for the men…and women that pick up a badge, put on a uniform, grab a gun, and stand a post. I will still hold doors and call you ma'am, not because you are less capable, simply because I'm old-fashioned and I believe I am being polite.

That being said, one of the more unique things that were brought to our attention was an unlicensed nightclub that was operating on Gwinnett Street. Now, I have to tell you, this one was different from anything I had ever seen. I remember when I first got back, on the midnight shift, there would be several cars parked along Gwinnett and Googe Streets mostly on weekends and into the very early morning hours. As observant as I like to think I am, I have to say I never even worried about it. I guess it wasn't what I was looking for but…

There was a legitimate bar that operated at Gwinnett Street very close to Styles Avenue. The owner paid liquor taxes, paid for liquor licenses, and abided by state laws about occupancy and operating hours. This other establishment did none of those things. Drugs, liquor, gambling, and whatever was all greenlit. It was called Woody's after the proprietor. Like everything else, if you want to make sure people are playing by the rules in a neighborhood, it has to be everyone, you can't just pick and choose. So we did the same thing at Woody's we would do at any crack house, we sent Ben in to buy a drink one early morning when bars are supposed to be closed. He got served, paid, and the transaction was complete.

We contacted the Georgia State Revenue Office and invited them along for a search warrant. When we executed the warrant, I couldn't believe my eyes. This was an actual nightclub. The structure was built off of what used to be a garage that the owner had made some interesting additions to. There were palm leaves attached to the walls and had a look like something you would expect to see in an episode of Gilligan's Island. There was everything you would expect in a nightclub, beer, liquor, mixers, a bar, mirrors and disco lights, tables, chairs, the works! The wiring and the old dry palm leaves made me wonder how this place didn't instantly ignite. I mean, the lighting, the stereo, the coolers, everything was all plugged into extension cords into the same outlets. A fire marshal's dream.

It was just one more thing we had to do to clean up the neighborhood, so we did it.

Sometimes, you just have to clean shit up

The city became a reliable partner in this operation. They weren't developing probable cause or identifying criminal activity but they were with us every step of the way. We called, they acted. I would drive down a street, see graffiti, and dial 311 and within hours, the graffiti would be gone. We would execute search warrants and they were there when we cleared to inspect the structure, and if they could condemn it, they boarded it up. If not, they identified the owner and the deficiencies to take enforcement action to clean up blight in the neighborhood. Ladonna Clark is the cousin of Syracuse basketball great Todd Burgan, a good friend of mine from our time at the New Hampton School. Ladonna was a former SCMPD Detective who worked for PMD at the time so our communication was easy. She was as helpful and valuable to this operation as anyone.

In the early 90's Savannah had its zenith of violence. The Ricky Jivens gang was active and the murder rate was out of control. Violent crime had risen by sixty-six percent from 1989 to 1991. Crack cocaine hadn't taken it easy at all on our quaint little city. A "weed and seed" program was started which, in a nut-shell was a community-based policing strategy. Officers working in the neighborhood and combating blight. We were not reinventing the wheel. This had been done but over time we had gotten away from it as an organization. Chief Lovett and Captain Thomas were younger officers and supervisors during the weed and seed program but they were more than familiar with what we were trying to accomplish. We didn't have to sell it or explain it or give it a name, we just had to do it.

Toby and I drove down Wexler Street. Toward the bottom of the neighborhood, there was an empty lot that had a house to the north and south of it. The grass had grown to nearly four feet high and as you can imagine, trash had built up in piles over a few years. A man was tending to his yard at his house just south of the overgrown lot. We stopped and looked at the growth and because I'm the funniest guy I know, I attempted to engage the man caring for his yard,

Why not just mow this one too? Pointing to the lot. Haha

In return, I got a disgusted stare and a quick head nod. Realizing I had hit a nerve and that this guy didn't think I was at all funny, I approached the man. I chuckled awkwardly and said,

Seriously, how long has this lot been like this? I asked.

They tore that house down two years ago and it ain't been touched since. He replied.

There was a pain in the way he answered. He was pissed. I thought about it and looked at his yard. Lawn mowed, bushes trimmed, not a speck of trash in the yard. A humble but well-kept home. It was obvious a lot of care and a lot of work had gone into the condition of this man's home. Toby has a way of putting people at ease. He started talking to the man and like he always does, disarmed him in a matter of minutes. He asked the man if he had ever called the city about clearing the lot. The look of disgust returned immediately.

I called those motherfuckers a year ago, they saw a car parked on my grass and wrote me a ticket. Then, they left and the lot still hasn't been touched. He snarled.

Imagine that. You painstakingly care for your home, an absentee landowner allows his lot to grow over, you call the city (government) to correct the problem, they arrive and take action against you for a seemingly minor offense and leave what you called about unaddressed. That would leave a bad taste in anyone's mouth. I could relate though. In my years of policing, I have seen it. A call for a drug complaint, dealers on the corner, and officers arriving and seeing the complainant having an illegally parked car and issuing them a ticket. It's a strange phenomenon, like a need to take enforcement action but on the wrong thing. Asking for help and getting kicked in the shin. I illustrate this to any young officers reading this, don't be a dick. These are the people who are trying to make their neighborhoods nicer to help you make them safer. It's a concept that doesn't show up in any training class and it shouldn't have to. You have to remember to be a decent human being before being a cop. It matters and it's important.

This was a no-brainer, we had to get this done. I told the man we would handle it. I got the same disgusted stare and the same head nod. We got in the car and I got on the phone. Savannah had a program called Savannah Impact (SIP). It was the police department working with probation and parole to help Probationers and Parolees get GEDs, develop work skills, and for some, provide jobs. One of the programs they had was a landscaping unit that could take care of this issue. I called and explained the situation, it started off well and they said it was definitely something they could do but it went south quickly. They couldn't tell me when and they wouldn't even consider doing it until they knew who was going to pay for it. Think about that, a police officer calling a unit in the same police department to help get a task completed and one unit wanting to know how the other unit was going to pay for it. Still think there is a thin blue line where cops cover up each other's shady behavior?

I hung up and now I was on a mission. It was about 9:30 in the morning and my blood was boiling. Carver Heights is in Savannah's first district. The alderman for District 1 in 2011 was Van Johnson. I called Van on his phone. We had met but I didn't know Counselman Johnson well. He was at the meeting with Dr. Temple and the Mayor when we presented S.A.R.G.E. to them. I told him about the lot and the conversation I had with the man on Wexler Street. Before I could finish my sentence Van Johnson said,

I'll handle it.

I'm not a huge fan of politicians but hell, I'll give anyone a chance to prove me wrong. Van Johnson was a supporter of EXPO when we were on the streets so I believed he understood.

Around three o'clock that afternoon, Toby and I went back into the neighborhood. We drove down Wexler Street and there was a crew of workers in the City of Savannah trucks, mowing and clearing the lot. I have a lot of friends who are not supporters of Van Johnson. I have had, and still have, some serious disagreements with Van Johnson on a lot of issues but I voted for Van Johnson for Mayor of Savannah in 2019. I will vote for him again because when I called him and needed him, he was there. I believe he was there not only because he understood what we were doing but because he actually cares about Savannah. (I just wish he would get rid of Roy Minter as Chief of Police).

As Toby and I rolled past, the man was standing in his yard with a rake, looking at the crew clear this lot. We rolled down the heavily tinted window and the man gave us a different stare and a quick head nod.

At one point later in the operation, we stopped when we saw the man in the yard again. We discussed all the activity that was going on in the neighborhood. He knew about the search warrants and had seen the arrests. This is a small community, people talk. We were finishing up our conversation when the man asked us,

So, y'all know about Barry and Lenny?

We were extremely aware of Barry and Lenny, two brothers who lived in their grandmother's house.

They keep their dope in the rafters in the carport over that station wagon. He said.

We told him we would see what we could do about that and drove off.

This will always stand out in my mind. Toby and I weren't acting as police officers, we were acting as decent men who were trying to help care for a neighborhood. We showed a man that no matter what his concern was that it mattered to us and more importantly, we would do something about it. He saw that we were men of action not just words. When we did for him, he did for us. That's how communities work. That's how police gain trust in communities. They say they are going to do something and they do it. You can't just say, "We need the community's help", and expect they will ever stick their necks out for you. We had already shown the neighborhood we were tough on drug dealers by kicking in doors and locking people up, the news showed this guy we cared about the neighborhood and tried to help him make his little corner of the world nicer. He responded by giving us what we needed to do the rest.

So here is one of my big problems with Chief Roy Minter and Savannah's City Hall. I guess it started back when Chief Lumpkin was Chief and Eddie Deloach was the Mayor but like the rest of America it became fashionable to adopt what is often called a "Hug a Thug" mentality and approach.

When "leaders" get up and say catchy things like, "If you see something, say something" or "We need the community's help" it shows they don't understand you need credibility to get people to trust you. You can go out and do all the nice handshakes and baby-kissing you want. That means nothing to people who are afraid to let their children play outside. If we had only cleared the lot, this man wouldn't have trusted we could actually get the criminals. He had already seen we were getting bad guys, the right bad guys, he knew we could and would do what we said we would do.

What's lacking today is the combined approach. The police have, sort of, stayed with the community outreach but have altogether stopped the enforcement strategies. Why? Because their Chief will turn on them the second anything goes even remotely wrong as in the case with Sergeant Mike Arango and Corporal Daniel Kang. The officers in Savannah have no faith in their Chief and are afraid that they might be next in his vendetta against anyone who opposes his agenda. So even if they were allowed to actually go out and aggressively police, there aren't many officers left with the ability to do it and the ones with the ability that are left are guarding their pensions, literally with their lives.

"We need the community's help" will continue to be answered with "Fuck you, do your job" but that doesn't alleviate City Hall's or the Chief of Police's responsibility to keep this Community safe. They are failing all of us but most of all they are failing the ones they are pretending to care about.

Parks were decorated with gang tags, S.A.R.G.E. made a point to get them removed.

Graffiti was removed and rarely came back.

We called and PMD came. Trash dumped was gone within an hour of the call.

It takes a village

Toby and I were starting to buy larger amounts of crack, the community functions were taking a lot of our time with Jack doing a lot of it and the paperwork was starting to pile up a little to where we needed to start taking administrative days to type reports.

We were identifying higher value targets but there were still complaints about drug houses in the neighborhood. There was an address on Griffin Street that was making people worry about what was going on back there. This was a job I would have loved to use Ben for but he had been ill so I wasn't exactly going to push him to "Work". So without an informant, we looked for the next best thing.

I would talk to a few of the go-getters on patrol that knew the area. I contacted Godfrey and asked him to stop anything he could coming or going to get some intel or try and get some dope that might lead us to a search warrant. If he could ID the guy who was supposed to be selling, that would be great too. I made the same pitch to two guys on the afternoon shift who were developing reputations also. Chase Cogswell and Rob Santoro. They were both relatively new to the department but I saw a lot in them. They were always after it and even if they were deterred by their leadership, they kept at it.

It wasn't long before all three of them made arrests of people with drugs coming from the house on Griffin Street. Kareem Robinson was supposed to be the dealer at this house and he was always armed according to the guys Godfrey, Santoro, and Cogswell had arrested. Without having to do a thing, purely on the good work and well-written reports these guys had made, I was able to get a search warrant for the address. Robinson was a convicted Felon and was on probation.

Having guys on patrol that could gather that type of intelligence was a huge asset. It was what we had hoped we would get from West Chatham's CSU but they showed very little interest. These three were top-notch guys.

We put together the PowerPoint, made the dots move, and hit the house early one morning. We woke Robinson up and found crack and a fancy .22 caliber pistol in his room. All this while we still were able to make buys and put sales cases because these patrol guys did everything we needed.

Godfrey, Santoro, and Cogswell were definitely the kind of guys that police departments need. Unfortunately, when you work for a department that has such a fucked up political climate, you lose guys like this to other agencies and even other careers. Godfrey left to work at a

Department near Atlanta, Cogswell made his way to CNT, The U.S. Marshals' Task Force, and eventually onto the ATF. He was a real lunkhead, a former Marine with a twisted sense of humor. The exact guy you would want in the foxhole next to you if shit ever hit the fan.

Then, there was Santoro. If I only got one word to describe this dude it would be driven. An over-educated, marathon running dynamo. We wound up working together in Homicide a couple of years later. Santoro had his own way of doing things and we would butt heads stylistically but I have to say this for the little guy, I have never seen anyone work harder than Rob Santoro (FYB). Working murders was in this kid's blood and his heart was pumping constantly. I have always been a huge fan of mine and prided myself on my work ethic but I have to tip my hat to Santoro, he had me and everyone else beat. Rob Santoro is the kind of cop no agency can afford to lose but Savannah lost him because of guys like Roy Minter. Hell, because of Roy Minter.

Toby would get letters of Commendation written for each of them from the ATF Special Agent in Charge of the Atlanta Field Division to go in their personnel files and he would give them challenge coins we had made for S.A.R.G.E. to give a little thank you for things exactly like what they had done for us. They were new at this point in their careers but it was easy to see they would do big things.

Top: Gun and crack cocaine recovered from Kareem Robinson's house that we wouldn't have gotten were it not for some young, aggressive officers' help.

Let's be honest

Probably the biggest problem we have in American society today is the ability to be honest and candid with each other and I find in many cases, ourselves. In my teenage years, I enjoyed being able to disagree with people. I used to love to argue, even if I didn't really feel the way I was arguing. I just liked to oppose what others were saying and I used as much info as I could get to make several frivolous points. In my house, disagreement was encouraged.

At least for me, I think things began to unravel around February of 2012 when a young man named Trayvon Martin was killed in Sanford, Florida. He was killed by George Zimmerman, a security guard under, let's just call them questionable circumstances. Trayvon's murder sparked outrage in the country that was reminiscent of murders like Medgar Evers and somehow put a spotlight on police in America. Remember, post 9/11, people loved the police. Then in 2014, Eric Garner was killed in New York City and Michael Brown was killed in Ferguson, Missouri by Officer Darren Wilson prompting an outcry against police brutality all over the country. Cities rioted as they had in the civil rights movement. Calls to demilitarize the police gained momentum and the phrase, "Hands up, don't shoot," and, "I can't breathe," played across our televisions in almost every forum imaginable. Athletes wore t-shirts with these themes on the national stage to protest racial injustice and brutality. Brutality and killing of black men by police became nightly news and continued in July 2016 when Alton Sterling was killed by police in Baton Rouge, Louisiana. Shortly thereafter, probably the biggest, most publicized, and the most polarizing protest took hold. A backup quarterback on the San Francisco 49ers knelt during the National Anthem. He wore socks that had the heads of pigs in police uniforms evoking the memory of Bobby Seale and Huey P. Newton's label for police when they formed the Black Panther Party for Self-Defense in Oakland California.

The country has been bombarded with case after case of police killing black men from 2012 up until February 2020 when Ahmaud Arbery was killed in Brunswick, Georgia by a former investigator for the Glynn County District Attorney's Office and Breonna Taylor was killed in Louisville, Kentucky during a search warrant in March 2020. Cries for demilitarization, defunding of police, diversity training among police, and police reform have become in vogue and seem to be a daily occurrence on major news stations, podcasts, films, and streaming platforms all over the country. So much coverage, so much attention, and such a big spotlight. It seems like police are running wild and killing black people all over the United States.

Again, let's be honest. Despite what we have been made to feel and regardless of how much of the national spotlight is put on the subject, the truth is, the American Police Officer is not the problem. Violent crime in America is on the rise. Gun violence is out of control and we are looking at the wrong issue.

I am not a sociologist, I don't put a lot of faith in the statistics that organizations present because I know they can be manipulated to say what you want them to say but I can tell you, without a doubt, that violent crime occurs in our poor communities. Poverty and lack of education are the root causes. Obviously, this is an oversimplified rundown of things but rather than wasting time talking about this study and that study let's just be honest. When I measure crime I look at how many people are murdered in non-domestic incidents and I look at shootings and street robberies. I am not dismissing, domestic crimes or property crimes or rapes, or assaults that don't involve firearms, they all count and have to be looked at. I measure safety simply as if an individual feels comfortable enough to travel around in a city, carrying a firearm, whether they are prohibited or not from possessing it, and have little fear of exerting their "Power" over others. When I worked the streets, these are the type of parasites I spent all of my uninterrupted time looking for. Drug dealers who trapped users then used guns to protect "their" territory or settled debts with other dealers. Gang members who are not afraid to pull guns on anyone who oppose them, and are willing to use them. They feel safe to operate and prey on our city when they are not policed - pure and simple.

The City of Savannah, Georgia makes its money on tourists. 2021 was a record-setting year for tax dollars in the tourist industry. While it wasn't a record year for murders, we did have more murders than in the previous four years and that trend continues. Savannah's city council is filled with people who campaigned on police reform. A task force was formed to get input from the community on police policy and our "action news" Aldermen and women show up on the scene to get to the bottom of police shootings and post it all on social media. The people who sit with the most influence over our city spend time and money looking at parking issues and trying to prevent traffic accidents all of which are important but don't even register on the social scale as a problem, especially when compared to the violence in this City. A police "Chief" who talks about combating "gangs, guns, and drugs" in our community, knows nothing about how to combat any of them. Yet, he still has a job and the perception is that there is no pressure on him to control crime. For decades, from the early 1990s until around 2012, the use of the word gang was forbidden in political circles in Savannah. I went into great detail about the amount of resistance officers got if they said they were investigating gangs or gang crime in my last book. Guys like Dave Dauphinee, Jose Ramirez, Steve Kholes, and Udon Carter caught a lot of flack. That was until there was a shooting at the City's Coastal Empire Fairgrounds in 2012. An incident of this magnitude happening at a place where there were so many people could not be ignored. Chief Willie Lovett and criminal District Attorney Meg Heap put on a united front and said gangs and gang prosecutions would be the priority. Truth be told, Willie Lovett had made gangs a priority years earlier. Operations like Raging Waters and Operation Ruffian were all geared towards gangs.

City Hall grimaced and prayed, but like most things in Savannah, time passed and few remember now what was set out all those years ago. What they did see however was even with gangs in the news, the tourists keep coming, students keep enrolling at one of the country's most prestigious art colleges and even Hollywood keeps coming to make movies. No news stories about the Mayor or City manager demanding answers or results in crime reduction. The days of Chiefs like David Gellatly, Dan Flynn, Michael Berkow, and Willie Lovett having to answer for high crime rates are gone. Concerns from Mayor Otis Johnson and Mayor Edna Jackson are gone. When Chief Lumpkin and Mayor Eddie Deloach took over there was no longer a huge concern. Mayor Deloach caught some flak from the Savannah Morning News but things were business as usual in the city.

People get killed, shot, and robbed in Savannah at an alarming rate and the tourists still come to see our beautiful city. Movies are made, and national attention is put on cases that feature beauty queens and debutantes but little attention is paid to drug dealers or poor people who are gunned down.

Instead, we focus as a city and as a nation on the evil police. People have been exposed to so much sensationalized media coverage they perceive and actually believe that police are killing people in record numbers.

In a nutshell, Treyvon Martin was not killed by police, Eric Garner had a heart attack while resisting arrest for a minor offense and his death could have been prevented if he had complied with Officers,

Michael Brown robbed a store, beat a police officer and was killed during the beating. Hands up, Don't shoot, never happened and Ahmaud Arbery was also not killed by police. So many other cases in which the facts were underreported, misrepresented, or not reported on at all have created this narrative that, let's face it, America wants to believe. It is simply not so. The mistrust that has been weaved into our society can't be undone. If a lie gets told enough that most people believe it, it's still a lie. Politicians are human and they are humans who need votes. If their constituents believe the police are a brutal murdering hoard hell-bent on the destruction of the black race then they have to represent those people and their beliefs. The number of people killed in this country by police in 2021 was less than one-third of one percent of the nation's population. About eleven percent of those killed were black. So about 113 people out of 1055. Now that's killed, not murdered. Doesn't seem like the genocidal pace getting portrayed on the news. The loss of one life is too many, especially if it is an unjustified killing by our law enforcement but if we compare it to the murders across the country, the police will not be your culprits. With approximately 20,340 murders in the United States in 2021, even if you look at justified police shootings as murder, the 1055 people killed by police are approximately five percent of those murdered.

The city of Chicago, arguably one of the most violent cities in the world which has affectionately been dubbed "Chi-Raq" had 795 people shot and killed in 2021. Nine of those were shot and killed by police. That's 1.2% of the killing in the city. (It is worthy to note that the nine police killings were all ruled justifiable). Simply put, if you want to solve the violent crime in the City of Chicago, going after the 1.2% will not be very helpful. So why is there such a big call for defunding and demilitarizing police departments nationwide? Why are we constantly bombarded with police killing black people seemingly indiscriminately if it is only five percent of the problem? Why aren't we more focused on the people who are committing the 95% of the murders in our country? I'll tell you why. We have been fed a load of shit in this country and many of us have chosen to believe it. "Hands up, Don't Shoot" never happened, yet it has been spread and covered by mass media. When it was proven to be false, it was not re-reported. No apologies for misinformation were broadcast. The seed was planted and will never be erased from our nation's memory. There will always be a portion of this country that believes Michael Brown was maliciously murdered by a police officer. It can never be undone and is just one example of what is helping to erode the fabric of trust between our nation's police officers and the public they serve.

If we stopped every single officer involved in a shooting that resulted in death we would accomplish nothing in relation to reducing violent crime in the United States. I'll repeat, the police in this country are responsible for approximately five percent of the people being shot and killed in this country and those are not murders! They are Officers putting their lives at risk to protect the public. For argument's sake, even if the police were murdering people at that rate (Which they aren't) why would we focus on five percent of the problem instead of the 95 percent?!?!?!?

The truth remains that in Savannah and much of the United States if it is only young black men being shot and killed, few people truly care. There were 34 people murdered in Savannah in 2021, 94 percent of those were black people. None of them were murdered by the police (There were two officer involved shootings and both were found to be justified by the GBI). Mayors, City Council, community leaders, regardless of their race simply don't care enough to do what is necessary if the bottom line is not affected. Plenty of other, less critical problems to focus on...ones with easier solutions.

It also pains me that while we focus on the false narrative of the police killing of black people, we ignore the rise of violence toward -

police in our country. Seventy-three officers were killed in felonious attacks (FBI via CNN) in 2021. When I began my police career in 1998, my only fear was being shot and killed. In 2021, 21 Officers were charged with crimes as a result of shootings that occurred in the line of duty in 2021 (NBC News). The bigger fear for police officers today is being indicted and sent to prison for performing their sworn duty.

Chief Willie Lovett and criminal District Attorney Meg Heap admitting publicly that there are gangs in Savannah, in 2012.

"It's my right...(of passage)"

I remember my first day at the Downtown Precinct. I had just been assigned to B Watch who, for this month, April 2005 were assigned to the midnight shift. I wasn't a full year removed from my service in the United States Army and I was still pretty uptight after having been through the paramilitary-style police Academy and five additional weeks of department training. Roll call was at 2330 hours at 201 East Lathrop Street. I showed up around 2230 hours just to make sure nothing would make me late...and, I was a little excited to get on the road and do some actual police work. I walked into the precinct, feeling special because I now had the access code to the building. Few lights were on because C Watch was out on the road and the last place your Sergeant wants you is away from your beat. I was early enough where people had not yet begun to sneak back in and no one from the next shift, except the brand spanking new rookie with his highly polished boots, would dream of being at work this early.

I was nervous but terribly excited as I rounded the corner into the area that was the roll call room. The lights were dim and only one row of fluorescent bulbs was turned on at the front of the room. The tables were lined up with chairs facing a podium and dry erase board. To my left were maps that showed the precinct's area of responsibility and what looked like the borders of each beat. A bold line outlined an area of the map and in the middle read "2-4", 2 being the precinct designation and 4 the beat number. I looked and started to imagine everything that was going on out there, I kind of got lost in all the action I was seeing in my head. I heard the sound of paper shuffling behind me. I was a little caught off guard because I didn't realize I wasn't alone. I had already failed to clear the room and in the immediate corner to the right of the entrance where sat Star Corporal Randy McCurry. Star Corporals were part-time supervisors in the department. If a Sergeant was not on shift or was otherwise detained, The Star Corporal would assume the Supervisory role if needed. In this instance, Corporal McCurry was reading and approving reports. I snapped to and out of reflex gave the Corporal the greeting of the day.

Good evening Sir, I said

Star Corporal McCurry fired me, what I now know was his famous look of disgust and replied simply...

Fuck you and went right back to what he was doing.

Now I'm not saying I'm old school police, I came along right as the whole feel-good about yourself movement was beginning but I had enough grit about me to know, I hadn't been around long enough yet to be welcomed. Especially not by someone who had been on the streets as long as McCurry. Nowadays I guess they call it hazing and would be an instant human resources complaint that might actually be listened to. I simply took it for what it was, a big dog letting a young pup know his place. This is one of the things that has evolved in the world of Law Enforcement. We are training Officers to be so sensitive to the needs of others that it has made them all too aware of their feelings. It used to be, you took a little shit, thickened your skin, and learned how to deal with a world that is not always friendly. It was a necessary part of the training and growing process in a Police Department. I am not in any way discrediting corporate strategies to make sure employees are being treated well and equitably. I have never been a huge fan of putting people down simply because they are new and inexperienced. In most scenarios, I don't even understand giving the new guys shit just because they are new. I will say though, Law Enforcement is a little different. Team building in an office is a little different than team building for the streets. There has to be a bond and a level of trust when all you do all day is go into unknown situations. The bond is not unlike that of a team in a contact sport where, if the man or woman to your left or right doesn't hold up their end of the task there is a possibility you could be hurt. In the police world, or "Copland" as my buddy Jay Dobyns refers to it, the stakes are a little higher. Now more than ever, mistakes on the street get cops killed.

I try not to be too dramatic about it all because, let's face it, the word hero has been devalued. During the pandemic, it seems that any act that exceeds sitting on your ass is being deemed heroic. I guess I'm old and grumpy but I'm not giving into that philosophy. I also don't think that simply because you wear a uniform or badge and carry a gun it instantly qualifies as such. I have fought in a war and I policed in a city that is dangerous, I am no hero. I've served with 1000's of men and women, I know very few honest-to-God heroes. There is nothing wrong with just being someone who goes out and does their job. No shame in performing your duty to your highest standard and calling it a day. There is satisfaction in a job well done. It doesn't always have to be extraordinary. Sometimes life is just life, work is just work and service is just that...service.

I had this conversation with my son, a newly anointed Soldier in the United States Army. Other than Father, Soldier is the title that I have held that I am most proud of. My son was telling me about discussions Drill Sergeants were having with recruits about individuals thanking them for their service. Since September 11th it has become commonplace for people to thank members of our armed forces for their service. In the days and years following America's greatest tragedy, I have heard so many different responses. I think "you're welcome" works just fine, but like everything else, many, including me, have put their spin on it. I reply "I'm glad they let me play but thank you". I say this because I have always looked at my service as something I was supposed to do. I didn't plan on being a Soldier but I knew from an early age I would serve other people. I always wanted to be the police as a kid and when I got older I began to recognize the service of our armed forces. I watched Operation Desert Shield and Desert Storm live on CNN and then, in college, I began to frequent VFW cantinas. I met and listened to Korean War and Vietnam War Veterans. I began to admire and respect them though I could not truly understand what they had done for me. Then, after college and my first ill-fated police job, I joined the Army. I was a proud member of the Charlie Company Comanches of the 795th Military Police Battalion and began to see there was something to this whole service thing, a proud tradition that dated back to 1775. I remember standing in Memorial Grove at Fort Leonard Wood, Missouri days before graduation from One Station Unit Training (OSUT) and being approached by my Commander, Captain Lorenzen. Lee Greenwood's

"God Bless the USA" was playing on the loudspeaker during our Distinct Unit Insignia (DUI) ceremony. This ceremony is where soldiers finish their Advanced Individual Training (AIT) and become soldiers in their chosen military occupational specialty (MOS), Military Police in my case.

"Moving, huh?" Said Captain Lorenzen,

I remember, like an idiot saying something to the effect of "sort of" because I was hung up on the song. I mean, "God Bless the USA " became the song I associate with the Gulf War…that was the best we could do? Look at Vietnam! The number of songs that come out of Vietnam. Songs by Dylan, Creedence Clearwater Revival, The Byrds, Buffalo Springfield, and so many more…now that was music. I was hung up on that and that alone. I remember the Captain looking at me disapprovingly. I didn't get it. At least I didn't get it at that time. I went on to the mighty 529th Military Police Company. The Honor Guard company for the United States Army Europe (USAREUR). That's where I learned about being a member of a Unit. That's where I learned about loyalty and it's where I learned about a right of passage.

I had a little rank when I got to my first unit. I was an E-4 Specialist because I had a four-year degree when I enlisted. I didn't know shit but I had a rank where I should be expected to have some pretty basic skills mastered. I didn't and I got shit for it. "InstaSpec", and "PV4" were a couple of the names I was called but I picked it up pretty quick, mostly because the 529th MP Company bred leaders and I had the privilege of serving with some of the best. Staff Sergeant Shawn Worley was my first Platoon Sergeant. The epitome of what a Sergeant should be. From the very first time we met until this day, I have always looked up to him. He was never my buddy though we have a strong personal relationship. He will always be my Sergeant. Years after I was out of the Army and after his retirement we spoke and I called him Sergeant. He told me to drop all that and call him Shawn. Roger Sergeant.

Leadership was a way of business in the 529th. If I list every Soldier I admire from that unit, this book will never end. For all my Honor Guard brothers and sisters, check the acknowledgments.

In August of 2018, Roy Minter arrived in Savannah and took the head spot in the Savannah Police Department. Since that time more than 306 Officers, including Sergeants have left. Just to put that in perspective. In three years, more than 300 Officers have left a department of just over 500. So they are replaced with new Officers.

That leaves more than 65% of the Officers in the Savannah Police Department with less than 3 years in the department. What kind of culture does that create?

The reasons for their departures vary but anyone with any contacts in the department can easily see "Chief" Minter is the reason. Roy Minter came from Peoria, Arizona. A city that continuously boasts that it is one of the safest cities in Arizona. In 2019, Peoria had 3 murders…little news flash Roy, this is Savannah, it's not safe here. Shootings in Savannah are commonplace and I hate to beat a dead horse but unless you are white or killed by police no one cares. The slogan "Come on Vacation, leave on probation" has been replaced by "That's just Savannah". The apathy of City government and the general public toward this level of violence is unforgivable. There were 23 murders in Savannah in 2019, Minter's first full year as Chief. The was down from 28 the year prior. Way to go! The problem is that the two years following saw a 47 percent increase in murders. 31 in 2020 and 34 in 2021. Pandemic? Who knows, I'll go with not knowing how to police a city that prides itself on its level of violence. No, you won't see travel magazines boasting how tough the streets of Savannah are, hell, you will barely see the local news coverage. If you are in or know the streets of

Savannah, you know, the rep of being a tough and violent city is thriving. The 912 or C-Port's reputation for being a city you don't come to fuck around in is alive and well.

Now, to be fair. I don't blame crime on the police. It is almost impossible to argue that the root causes of crime are not poverty and lack of education. No doubt, that's the cause. America's success has made many feel college is the only path to success and the nation has geared its entire education system to try and make every peg fit in every hole. Aside from losing what is truly special about America, this practice is also discouraging to students and kids who just aren't cut out for that path. Discouraged kids drop out of school, find little reward in menial tasks and are inculcated into the street life that they see glamourized in movies and music…ok, sociology lesson over. My point is the police are not to blame for the crime problem until they do not combat it effectively.

So, who do we hold accountable for that? I blame the Chief. The top guy. The face of the department. His strategy and culture are what shapes how a police department functions. I'll go back to a point I tried to make in my first book; there is a big difference between a cop and a career police officer. Cops know how to deal with crime. Career police officers are better with the administrative side of things. Roy Minter is a career police officer, and not a very good one. He came to a department that is well known for its internal unrest and found a way to make it worse. I've heard many people suggest that money is the solution to retention problems. While there is no question that more money makes things more livable I argue that it does little for satisfaction. Going to work every day and risking your safety for the good of others isn't a mission that gets measured in dollars and cents. It's the kind of thing a cop does because it's inherent in the make-up of who they are. There is no price tag for it. It is a call to service and a feeling of belonging to a tribe responsible for safety. A cause that is for the greater good. In 2022, it seems funny to say that because police have been villainized in mass media but truly, the police are there to help. To keep the public safe. That is the mission. Without the support of strong leaders, who will stand with you when you have to make unpopular decisions, use force, and even take a life. the system breaks. Cops don't stick their neck out and ultimately, the bad guys win.

A different way of doing shit

In June, things were hitting pretty good. Search Warrants had been successful and I felt pretty comfortable at this point saying that if things were happening in Carver Heights, we knew about it. We might not be able to immediately act on it but we had plenty of resources we could turn to. To me, that was the eventual goal of the operation. I wanted to know what was going on in every neighborhood in Savannah. It was right around this time that the department was trying to put together a twenty-man, street-level drug squad. Not exactly like EXPO and not exactly like CNT. This unit would work street-level drugs and get search warrants much like the ones we did with Tang and Sandman. A combination of crime suppression and drug work. I couldn't help but think that if they just added 4 investigators to S.A.R.G.E., the right four investigators, then we would have what we needed and more. If I covered two or three neighborhoods and a guy like Castro could cover two neighborhoods, then when it came time to do buys, jump-outs, or serve warrants we could use CSU for whichever precinct we were and we would have enough personnel. Then they could go back to whatever they were doing when we were done. That's a five-man unit assigned to the intelligence center gathering and acting on intelligence as things developed. That way the intel all goes back to the intelligence center and can be controlled and distributed along with personnel not being tied up on temporary assignments that hurt their numbers. Just a thought but again, I didn't have a lot of juice.

Nick Melke, who started with Metro right about the same time I did, was a West Chatham Precinct Detective. He saw Toby and me one day and said he needed a favor. There was a burglary out on Little Neck Road where more than 10 guns had been stolen. He had a few leads but nothing really solid to go on. His suspect was a kid who lived in Carver Heights and he hoped some of the guns were at his house. Melke definitely didn't have enough for a search warrant. The thing about guns is you have to get to them fast if you have any idea of where they are. Guns go quick on the street because no one wants to get caught in possession of them and even worse, no one wants rivals coming and taking them, that can get ugly. Remember, on the street guns are what get you "real" time in prison. I had no idea who this kid was and when we looked, it wasn't much of a criminal history. Willie Knight was under our radar, but Melke had just put him on it. Guns in the neighborhood we were trying to get guns out of? Sure, we'll go talk to him.

Melke gave us the address and we went and did a "knock-and-talk". No probation, no 4th amendment waiver so we were going to need this kid to give us consent if we wanted to search and that takes some smooth-talking at least if you were dealing with experienced criminals. We were lucky, this dude was anything but experienced. We approached the house just as a young man, matching the description Melke gave us exited the house. He had a backpack and looked like he was going somewhere. We got to the stairs just as he was turning from closing the door.

What's up, man? How you doing? I asked

Who me? the young man replied.

I always loved that response. "Who me?" There is no one else on the porch and a very clearly labeled policeman walks directly up to you, with a guy he came with, and asks you, "What's up?" Who the fuck else do you think I'm talking to? But, that's probably the most common answer from anyone I have ever approached that was up to no good. Dollars to doughnuts, he would respond "Huh?" to anything I asked him after.

"Are you Willie Knight?" I asked…

"Huh?" he replied

The next most common response to a question that is asked of someone who is up to no good. A person's conscience has a funny way of deceiving them. Telltale signs of wrongdoing. Cops who have been on the street, especially in the neighborhoods where drugs are prevalent recognize these responses after years and thousands of street interviews. Josh Hunt and I used to have so much fun with these little exchanges,

"Who me?" The subject would ask…

"No, him"… Hunt would say turning to me, *"do you have anything on you that you wish you didn't have?"*

"Huh?" I would respond, turning back to the subject

"Huh?" the subject would say.

And around and around we would go. It's almost a script that cops and criminals follow on a daily basis. The more people you stop and talk to the more familiar you get with your lines and expect certain responses from your castmates. I've stopped and talked to thousands of people. I knew where this conversation was going.

Willie Knight was not a smooth guy. He began to stutter, he began to sweat. He gave every physiological sign of stress that I had ever read about, been trained on, or witnessed from someone who was in possession of something they should not have been. I knew it, Toby knew it and so did Willie. We didn't have to talk long. Willie sat on the porch with us and we explained to him the gig was up. He had given himself away. Willie had seen what was going on in the neighborhood and he had seen all the doors getting kicked in and people getting charged federally. Willie wanted no part of that.

Toby leaned in as only Toby could do and asked,

"Any of them guns on that house, Dawg?" Willie just nodded.

"Alright Beau, take us to them?" Toby asked

Again, Willie just nodded. We all stood up and Willie went to pick up his backpack. I told him just to leave it there, we would get back to it in a few minutes. Willie stared at that bag like it had gold in it. Guess what? It didn't.

Willie took us to the closet in the house. Pointed to a vacuum cleaner and told us to open the dust flap where you clean everything out, and there it was, a 1911 style pistol, one of the ones stolen in the burglary. Of course, we asked if there were any other guns in the house and Willie said there weren't. I believed him but I knew Melke would want to see for himself and probably would want to get a warrant to search everything else. He had all the probable cause he needed at this point to get one. We called Melke and told him we found one of his guns and waited for him to arrive.

We sat back down on the front porch and Willie's eyes were glued to his backpack. He wouldn't even break his gaze as we made small talk and explained that Detective Melke was on his way. We told him that because he had been so cooperative, we wouldn't present any charges he had to the Federal Grand Jury, which was true because, with no criminal history, he wasn't going to meet the guidelines for federal prosecution anyway. None of that broke his laser focus on his bag. Toby and I kept looking at each other, smirking, waiting for the other one to ask. Finally, Toby leaned in,

"There's another gun in that sack ain't there? Toby asked.

You could see the life drain from his expression, Willie nodded and said we could grab it if we wanted to. We definitely wanted to. We pulled a Desert Eagle out of Willie's backpack. Now, I don't think Willie had the kind of heart to use that hand cannon but I'm damn sure it didn't get in the hands of someone who might.

Melke showed up and took it from there. Melke didn't have to come to us. He could have worked the case a hundred other ways. A lot of people don't ask for help because of ego. Melke didn't have one. He had a case, thought we might be able to help and we did. That in turn helped us show Command Staff that we were a valuable asset to the rest of the department and the S.A.R.G.E. was an effective tool. Sergeant Mike Nichols, the Sergeant of Detectives in West Chatham would take notice.

The kind of firepower we wanted out of the neighborhood.

It was about that time that Sergeant Nichols came to me and said he needed something. SGT Nichols was the Detective Sergeant for the West Chatham Precinct and when I say Sarge was an old school cop, Sergeant Mike Nichols was the textbook definition of old school cop. His gruff exterior made him seem unapproachable, his thundering bark on a scene left no doubt who was in charge all on top of a reputation that he would give his own mother a ticket if she ran a stop sign. He also had the reputation of a bruiser, a guy you didn't fuck with on the street. Old School.

Sergeant Nichols had an address and some information that stolen property was being stored and fenced from a house on Carr Avenue. Directly across the street from Tang's old house. He asked me if I would look into it and see if I could get in there. I have to tell you, If Mike Nichols didn't think I was a good cop, he would not have wasted his breath asking me anything. It was one of the ultimate compliments of my career to have an old-school guy like Sergeant Nichols have any confidence in me.

The amazing coincidence was that we had just sent Charley to buy dope from that very same address earlier that day. I didn't have a warrant yet, so I waited to tell him but when I got it signed the next day, I called Sergeant Nichols and told him I had a search warrant for the house on Carr.

Bullshit, he said.

No sir, plan on hitting it Friday morning if you want to come. I said.

Aright, he said with a chuckle.

It was a proud moment for me. To have a guy I respected, have enough respect for me to ask me to look at something and to be able to produce immediately. I love it when the chips fall into place. I'd rather be lucky than good any time.

We executed the search warrant the same way we did all the others. Because we were going for drugs and because Ben told us that the target was armed during the buy, S.W.A.T. led the way. They flash-banged the bedroom and broke the glass in the window. The target ran through the glass and cut his foot. He was taken into custody and when I finally entered the house, there were all kinds of things in the living room. SGT Nichols and one of his detectives came in and he just grinned. I was as happy about seeing that grumpy old man grin as I was about finding the cocaine and the pistol our target had slid on top of the cabinets. It was a success all the way around.

Gun and drugs we recovered from the house on Carr Ave.

Same guys, doing the same shit, in the same place

Around December, with the feeling we had proven our point in Carver Heights, Chief Lovett wanted us to move into Cuyler-Brownsville (CBV). Except Hitch Village, Cuyler-Brownsville was my favorite neighborhood to police in. CBV sits between MLK Boulevard and Ogeechee Road on Savannah's west side. It goes from Anderson Street to Victory Drive. The "Dirty '30s" are a rough area between Anderson and West 37th Street but the real heart of CBV is from West 38th Street to West 42nd Street and spans from the 500 Block all the way to Ogeechee Road. This is home to some real criminals. Crips, real gangsters who are proud of the amount of violence they create. I'm not going to teach a gang lesson here but it is important to know. Savannah's gangs are real with national ties but neighborhood loyalty will trump any outside gang or organization, including the police. I guess you may just have to take my word for it but ask any cop where the real criminals in Savannah are from and I guarantee Cuyler-Brownsville will be at the top of the list.

I wasn't surprised the Chief sent us that way, I was excited. I knew a lot about CBV from my EXPO days and Jack knew it because he had come from Central Precinct but Jack would step into the role as the department's gun detective because Capers, as we suspected, had been promoted back to Sergeant and been assigned to the West Chatham Precinct. He would keep an eye on our progress from there but would not be involved in our day-to-day.

Jack and I had arrested, chased, and followed just about every criminal in CBV back in 2006 and when we drove through in 2011, nothing had changed. Same guys, doing the same shit, in the same place.

Toby and I pulled into the neighborhood and I toured him to the hotspots. The Dips at 38th and Bulloch, 42nd and Harden, the 600 blocks of 40th and the epicenter of it all, 39th and Burroughs.

Back in 2006, this whole area, at least the street level, was run by a guy named Amhud Dickerson a.k.a. Mhud. Mhud would post religiously on Burroughs Street, just south of "the 9". He would always be there and during our EXPO days, he would run us ragged. I can't tell you how many times foot chases were initiated after Maud and if we're being honest, he won a lot more than he lost. He was fast but more importantly, he was smart. If my guess was correct, it was still his show and the cast of characters would be similar to what it was back then.

I saw Maud as we drove through and I pointed him out to Toby.

It starts with him, anything going on here, goes through him. I told him.

Captain Ben Herron was the Precinct Commander when we first got the word that we would shift but in January, a round of promotions would take place that would change the game completely. Captain Devon Adams would be moved to Central Precinct as the Commander and he would assign newly promoted Sergeant Josh "J Murder" Hunt to take over the Crime Suppression Unit from Sergeant Ashley Brown, another Savannah legend.

Devo is a real cop. Savannah born and bred and no stranger to the real crime in the city. I first met Devo when he was the Lieutenant over Violent Crimes. He was always straight up with me and I respected him. I didn't know anyone on Central's CSU because they were all new, young hard chargers but I knew if J Murder was their Sergeant and Devo was their Precinct Commander, they were going to do exactly the type of damage we would need them to do.

There was a unit that was already doing some work in CBV that was called COTU (Career Offender Tracking Unit) There were two guys assigned to it and they had already got some guns and made some arrests of guys we had identified. We took a look at some of the cases they made and we started out getting those pushed to the United States Attorney's Office.

Homicide SGT Rob Gavin called me when he heard we were heading into CBV and asked me to come along on a search warrant they were executing on the 500 block of West 40th. Gavin was an old school cop, a guy I looked up to. He was the Sergeant in Homicide and Detective Nathaniel Kirkland III was the lead on this murder. Nate the Great and I worked together when I was a rookie and he remains the most thorough and professional Officer I have ever worked with. The murder involved a couple of guys who were on our radar also but I didn't know a lot about them.

S.W.A.T. hit the door and found a bunch of Marijuana and some cocaine as well as a few items of interest in the murder. I took over the drug evidence while Nate the Great focused on the important stuff. I got some great intelligence and it got the ball rolling before we had the lay of the land. The irony is that the suspects in this murder would wind up being extremely important to the case we would soon be making.

As we rounded the corner, one of my favorite kids from the old days was standing at the corner of the nine and Burroughs. Just chilling. We stopped and got out to say hello.

Oh shit! Wassup G? Charlton Reagan a.k.a. Midget greeted me.

What up Midge? I replied as we gave a dap hug.

Midget was a terror as a younger kid and possibly the fastest criminal I have ever chased. In 2006, he was always down at "the Dips" but it was clear he was holding this corner now. I introduced him to Toby and as always, they got along fine. There was nothing official about this visit. We were, seriously, just saying hello. We talked about how things were going and we exchanged pleasantries. The whole time, Midget was trying to feel me out for why we were there. I let him know.

Bruh, I need you to feel me on this, I said. *I need you to stop doing what you're doing.*

Man, you know how it is, my name rings out in these streets, he deflected.

My man, I feel you but I need you to feel me on this, you gotta stop, I warned.

For real, I ain't doin shit, ask Hunt, he be seein me all the time, Midget protested.

I can only put it to like this, stop or the only thing I can do is put you in prison. I told him.

He just nodded, gave me a dap hug and Toby and I left. I was hoping Midget would heed my warning, realize I wasn't playing and the error of his ways, and go do something else. It wasn't probable but I hoped. I think it gets lost when the general public sees police interactions in real life or in TV and film. Some of us genuinely like these guys. We see promise and get to know them on a little deeper than a surface level. Later in my career when I was in Homicide, after an interview with a young man I had known since I started on my beat in Hitch Village, a colleague of mine said,

You really like these guys don't you? He asked in wonderment.

Some of them, yes, I liked and cared about many of them. I don't think that sentiment is uncommon. If you work in a neighborhood for any amount of time and deal with individuals repeatedly, it's not unlike going to an office or factory and dealing with co-workers. In the projects and neighborhoods like Cuyler-Brownsville, it was the same people, in the same place, doing the same thing. I met a cast of characters in my career and I watched how they interacted with different officers. The ones who liked me, the ones who couldn't stand me, and all the ones in between. It was an interesting observation of the human dynamic. Some of these guys could have been anything they wanted to be in different circumstances but in the ones they were in, they chose to be criminals and they were serious about it. Like them or not, we would have to do something about it.

We were going to go at CBV differently than we did Carver Heights because even though it was only a short distance away, it was an entirely different world. These were a different, far more violent breed of criminal. We showed our hand the entire time we were in Carver Heights, in CBV we would have to play chess with a bunch of Jokers who loved the challenge. We would give them enough to make them wonder what we were doing but when we let them know, it would be too late. We would have them wrapped up. I had given Midget his warning, it was up to him to share it. Like I said, the only thing I could do to stop it was put him and anyone else who was making CBV a dangerous place in prison. Something had to change so we couldn't allow the same people, in the same place to do the same thing.

One of the cool things about working with the Feds is that they generally have access to some of the cooler gizmos you can use in an investigation. I mean, sometimes it takes them a while to get them but when they do, they have the budget for the good stuff.

I remember the first time I ever sent an informant to buy dope with the ATF's equipment during Operation Raging Waters and let's just say, I was less than impressed. They mic'd the guy up with a recorder that was basically the size of a VHS tape. Now, however, they had dropped a few pennies to get us some good stuff. When we wired Ben up the first time, the audio recorder was not a lot bigger than a credit card. Little thicker but easy to hide. For Christmas though, Belsky got us the ultimate gift. An interception device that recorded audio and video. I won't go into exactly what the device was because I'm sure it still gets used every now and again today but man, you could hear and see everything the informant did. The first problem is that it only recorded, it didn't transmit. So we would wind up using a combination of devices. One transmitted and recorded audio and the other recorded audio and video. The next problem was that it only had a limited battery power so from the time you turned it on, you had 45 minutes to go, do the deal, and come back so we could see everything. Still, having video was a game-changer.

We were going to take a different approach in CBV. We knew the areas where dope was being slung like it was legal and we knew who was slinging it. The problem for us was saturation and how were we going to specifically target individuals. The thing with Cuyler-Brownsville is that these were a very different kind of criminal. These guys had a very little social media profile. We knew who they were from years on the street dealing with them. The only real resume you would find on the majority of the guys was a criminal record. We had a list and a link chart that I put together from police reports and associations. We hung it on the wall in the office and we went to work.

We grabbed Charley and drove to a spot on the outside of the neighborhood. Trust me, if anything that doesn't look right rolls into CBV, the neighborhood knows. Especially the 600 blocks of 38, 39 and 40th Street. It's a tight-knit area and it's one that these guys don't leave. Seriously, some of them have never left the neighborhood for anything except school, jail, or a hospital.

Charley didn't have a driver's license so we had to get creative. We got a bike from the property room and signed it out before it was going to be auctioned. Charley was cool with it and agreed it played well because it's easier to get away and hide shit from police on a bicycle. On a bike, you can fit in tight spaces, get around a corner and lose whatever is on you. A bike draws a lot less attention than a car also. No equipment violations or seat belts and it is easy to explain just riding through all you have to do is ride on the correct side of the street and you're golden.

We met just south so there wasn't a far ride, again, we were worried about the time frame. We would do all the things we needed to do, wire Charley up, and send him on his way. We never told him where we would be during the deals but we would follow from a distance so we could monitor the wire but we didn't want to get too close. Police presence, as much as we like to fool ourselves, really didn't deter any activity in CBV. They were so used to seeing a police presence, they learned how to work around it. Toby and I in an unmarked though would make people wonder what was going on so we stayed on the outside of the neighborhood but close enough that we could get there fast if something went down.

We had a cover team stay on the outskirts too and we would radio when the informant was in the Area of Operation (A.O.). For this one, we sent Charley to the 600 block of West 40th Street with $100 to fish and see who would bite. Charley rode in, we heard some conversation, and he rode back out. When we saw him head out MLK, we went back to our agreed-upon meeting place. Charley rolled up a few minutes later and we grabbed the recorders and he handed us a good chunk of Crack Cocaine.

Charlie told us he rode down the street and there was only one guy posted. As Charley rode by him, they made eye contact and the guy gave him a head nod.

What you need? The man asked

A yard... Charley responded.

Hard? He asked.

Yup.

The man went into the front door of a house and came out with a big chunk of Crack and placed it in Charley's hand as Charley handed him $100. Of course, it was in $20's, $5's, $10's, and ones because no one buys street-level drugs with $100 a bill, except the police. Then Charley rode straight back to us. That was the story and we now had a chunk of crack cocaine or "hard" as it is called on the street. Crack is hard as opposed to cocaine powder which is "soft". I'll let you figure that out on your own. Charley told us how it went down to include the address of the door he went into. They didn't exchange names or numbers, it was just a smooth deal.

We loaded up the bike and dropped Charley back near where he was staying and we went back to the office to download the wire and the new recording device. This would be the first test of this device and I got to tell you, we were pleased. The video was clear and the audio was perfect. We could see and hear the exchange happen exactly as Charley had described. The dealer's face was clear as a picture in the video and I was able to take a screenshot of it for the report. It was a face I knew. He wasn't on our list already but I was sure I knew who it was that had just bit and entered himself into our game. I turned to my computer and pulled a picture up from the jail booking system. Yup, no doubt, Vincent Holbrook. I hadn't had too many run-ins with Vincent, mostly because he was locked up for most of the time I was running around CBV with EXPO. I would later show the still shot to Glenn Castro, who was a Central Precinct guy and knew everyone in this neighborhood. No doubt it was Vincent. The address also came back to Vincent's mother. This was by far the clearest sales case I had ever made. We watched it like we were there. You could see his face, you could see him take the money and you could see him put a white chunk in Charley's hand. Plus, you could watch the ride in and back out and see that Charley didn't stop and talk to anyone. As soon as a defense attorney saw that video, it would be a guaranteed plea deal. We would send Charley back to fishing in a day or two and Vincent would step back up and sell Charley more Crack.

It's that simple. Two deals and a criminal history and you're going to federal prison. So our fishing expedition worked and now we had a recipe to follow. We were off to a good start. So we would just keep going to the honey hole and see what, or more importantly who we could catch.

Another piece of technology we had continued to pay off for us back in Carver Heights too. We had hidden a surveillance camera at the corner of Styles Avenue and McCarthy Street to keep an eye on things. This camera was fantastic because we could link to it and watch what was happening from our laptops.

One night, Toby couldn't sleep so around 1:30 a.m. he logged in and saw our old friend Bookman posted on the corner with a buddy or two. Now, we had been out of the neighborhood for a little while but they didn't know that. So Toby called Bookman on his cell phone,

Hello? Bookman answered

Dawg, what are you doin' on the corner this late? Toby asked

There was no need for Bookman to ask who it was, Toby has a voice that is not mistaken for anyone else on the planet. The slow drawl that could only come from a boy from Dixie-Union, Georgia.

Ain't shit, just chillin', Bookman said. Now looking around to see where Toby was watching from

Where you at? Bookman asked.

Bruh, I'm everywhere and you should probably go inside, Toby told him.

With that Bookman and his buddies turned around and walked right down McCarthy Street and went in for the night. That was about the only advice Bookman took. He was another one we spent some time with to try and persuade to get out of the game. We heard he had moved onto Googe Street and started dealing deeper in the neighborhood. So like trusted public servants, true to our word, we dealt with that too. We would make two sales cases and remove Bowman from the neighborhood at the end of the operation.

So we wound up fishing the next day. We sent Charley in and he met someone new on the same block. Now Charley wasn't from CBV but he knew the game well enough to make some smaller buys. Plus, he had made some buys from a guy on the block and been seen and no one went to jail. In the dope world, everyone is suspected to be police. Dealers are paranoid but once they see you are in the game and that no one gets hauled off right away, their guard comes down. I mean it basically boils down to making money. There is risk involved but if they have any reason to believe their customer is legit, they will make a sale.

Charley came back to us and said he met a new guy who called himself Ced. Charley handed us the dope and told us how the deal went. He said Vincent wasn't out there and we didn't care. We had everything we needed from Vincent so we preferred not dealing with him again. We wanted more people to remove from the block when it came time to sweep them up. So, like we always did, dropped Charley off and went to find out if the deal went the way he said it did. You have to understand, an informant can tell me how a deal went down and every time I'm going to check behind him to make sure it couldn't have happened any other way. The video made that so much easier for us because it was almost like we were along for the ride.

Sure enough, it was just like Charley said. He rode in and there was a guy about mid-block. He rode past like he was looking for Vincent and the guy waved and asked,

What's up? The man asked

I'm lookin' Charley responded.

How much you need?

A yard Charley told him,

A'ight, bet the man told him

The man pulled out a baggie from his pocket and broke a chunk off of a larger rock and handed it to him and took the money.

*Yeah man, I seen you around, I'm Ced if you need more…*he said

These are the conversations that were damning. Here you have a guy, partially identifying himself, offering to sell more drugs. Imagine how that would play in front of a jury. Seeing the deal happen right in front of you and hearing their offer to sell the informant more. Evidence like this makes the defense of trying to make distorted audio sound like he said something else or, it was one-time thing seem kind of absurd.

I had never seen this guy before so we would need some help identifying him. I took another still shot from the video and printed it out. I showed the pic to some of Hunt's younger guys but they didn't know who this guy was. I turned the corner and saw Castro,

Know this cat? I asked.

Castro grinned his Pepe' Le Pew smirk

*Cedrick Henderson…you need to get back in them streets…*He laughed.

Glenn Castro was the real police. He always had a feel for the key players in any neighborhood but he learned how to police in Central Precinct and if you wanted to be any good at it, CBV was the place to learn and Castro was the expert. I always appreciated his help, he didn't have an ego. A lot like Rufus Brown in that respect. They would help you because they wanted to see the bad guys go away. They didn't care about who got credit for what, they just wanted the job done.

Cedrick Henderson had an impressive record. We would make a couple of buys from him over the next week and he would talk about being on Probation and more identifiers to make our job easier. More evidence that if he went to trial on the charges there was no doubt that it was him and that he was selling drugs.

I've mentioned this a couple of times. It might sound like I was afraid to go to trial but nothing could be farther from the truth. I loved going to trial. I loved making a case that could not be defended and I loved seeing the prosecutors put all the pieces together. Toby and I didn't make cases hoping for plea deals but we were thrilled when they happened because we knew it was because our cases were solid and these guys couldn't risk going to trial or else they would face far stiffer penalties. Make no mistake, for the cases we were taking federal they were stiff enough but if they fought them, they would get buried.

In an oversimplified summary, when people call for reform in the criminal justice system I think this is where it needs to be. Cases get pled to keep the system moving. If every case went to trial, the backlog would stall the entire system to a point where it would no longer be productive. People who did not have a bond would sit in jail awaiting trial for years and regardless of their probation or parole status would be incarcerated without having been found guilty. That violates everything that our system stands for. If District Attorneys and Public Defenders Offices don't find some compromise, and prosecutors and defense attorneys don't work out plea deals for cases, the system halts. This is exactly what has happened in Chatham County Georgia. The system is at what seems like a complete stop. With over 28,000 cases backlogged and awaiting adjudication, it makes it nearly impossible to get closure to these cases. With a new District Attorney who is not afraid to make the tough calls, however, there is some hope. Cases like the one made against SGT Mike Arango, for purely political reasons need to be disposed of expeditiously. Just an opinion but if cases are not based on actual criminal statutes and solely on a trend that tries to paint police as criminals, they need to go away.

The other huge plus of cases that didn't go to trial is we had a lot more time on the street. Cops tied down in court hearings take them away from the mission. The courtroom stuff is as necessary as the work itself but if you make cases strong enough that they don't need you in court, you have more time to crush it on the street.

So why aren't all cases made on video? Hell, I wish it was that easy. We had a piece of equipment that fit into what we were doing perfectly and it allowed us to get this evidence. It doesn't always work like that. Clothing, accessories, and items that have been turned into these recording devices become known, the clothes go out of style, it is a constant cat and mouse game and then whatever is in fashion becomes a race to get it made and out onto the street. The device also has to fit the person that is wearing or carrying it. I guess the only way I can say it is that you don't want a device that stands out in any way or calls attention to itself. As soon as it is noticeable, it is no longer worth the risk to the informant or the undercover.

So we kept fishing. We sent Charley in every couple of days at different times to try and buy from different individuals. We made the buys and identifications the same way. He'd come back, give us the crack, we'd review the video, compare it to Charley's account and we would ID the guy off the video.

One such expedition got us very excited. A shot at the top dog. Charley came riding in and Mhud was sitting on a stoop at 39th and Burroughs. Right where he used to always be. Amhud Dickerson was the poster child for this operation and Charley was riding straight towards him. When Charley got close enough Mhud looked up and waved him off, shaking his head and gesturing towards one of the younger guys on the street. Our hopes were dashed. That is as close as we got Amhud Dickerson. Could we have made an intelligent argument based on our training and experience that he was a party to the crime? I suppose. The fact that he acknowledged the buyer, shook his head no was clear that he knew the buyer was there for something and the clear gesture to someone else who provided the buyer with crack cocaine could be articulated as being party to the crime. I have to admit, for a second, I thought about it but there is no fucking way I was going to charge Amhud Dickerson on some trumped-up minor league drug charge. If we were going to get him, it was going to be the right way. Charging him for something like this would be exactly the kind of case you would pray he would plea to. It was a defensible charge. An argument could be made that he didn't know the guy approaching him and he shook his head telling him to get away from him. I could have argued his history and how I know his association with all these younger guys and it was him directing a drug buyer to a drug dealer to make a transaction. I couldn't however prove or even explain how Mhud would have benefitted from this transaction or if the younger guy paid Mhud for what was sold. I had strong confidence in that this is exactly what was going on but confidence is not proof. There was no way I was going to charge the guy we wanted most with such a humble charge. I had chased this guy too many times earlier in my career to not have the charge stick. That's not what Toby and I were about.

The ironic thing about this is that Amhud Dickerson would be prosecuted under Operation Ruffian, just not for a case Toby and I made.

Maud got stopped one early afternoon by Ron Tyran. Tyran was at CNT for most of the time I was at Metro but was now back on patrol. He stopped Mhud for a traffic violation and it turned out Mhud had been drinking. Tyran, having been a cop and worked dope for so long probably didn't want to get tied up on a DUI stop so he asked Mhud if there was anyone who could come get him. An acceptable way to deal with the situation. Mhud said he would call his sister and Tyran went and checked Mhud info. Again, being an experienced drug investigator, Tyran found that Mhud was on probation for some serious drug charges and had a 4th amendment waiver. Tyran approached Mhud and asked him to stand up. He explained what he had found out and asked if there was anything in the car he needed to know about…

Mhud was one of the fastest and smartest guys I had ever dealt with on the streets, he turned away from Tyran and placed his hands in the small of his back in handcuffing position, and said,

Yeah man, look under the seat

Amhud Dickerson didn't run, didn't fight, and just surrendered. There was a stolen pistol under the seat. I was shocked but at the same time, I appreciated the irony. Maybe he was just tired of the game or maybe, if we had just given him a few drinks all those years ago we would have been able to catch him. I like to think though that maybe he just grew out of the game. I have bumped into a few of his acquaintances over the past year and they say when he got home he went straight, owns a house, and has a family. I hope that's true because I always kind of liked the guy.

We adopted the case because he was the main target of the second half of our operation but Ron Tyran made the case and deserves all the credit.

Coming up big

We were getting all the drugs we wanted and were racking up a number of defendants. Vincent and Ced were two of the bigger guys with longer histories and we were able to buy from Anthony Williams a.k.a. Trunk who was a particularly violent guy from the neighborhood. We also made some small deals from some of the younger guys just to make it seem like Charley didn't have any particular favorites.

We had Charley feel some of these guys out to see if anyone was selling pistols. Drugs are one thing but guns are something entirely different. Anyone going in buying drugs for real isn't going to be very picky about who they get them from but you have to be extra careful if you are buying guns. People selling guns are a whole lot more careful because with guns, come the Feds.

We started to direct Charley to go into the neighborhood from different directions so he could run into different people. That's when we bumped into "Chill". He was not someone I had ever seen at 38th and Burroughs. He was walking down the street as Charley rode in and flagged him down.

You lookin'? Chill asked

Yeah, I need...

Before Charley could finish, Trunk came from around the corner and yelled

You tryin' to blade my play?!?!

*Nah...*Chill replied and walked off telling Charley his phone number

Charley went and made the deal with Trunk to keep things cool. Now, I have to admit, I was unfamiliar with the terminology "Blading my play" but it was clear that Trunk, who had been on this corner for as many years as I could remember didn't appreciate anyone trying to make a sale on his corner. It was also clear that Chill wanted no part of Trunk.

We would contact Chill a day later and set up a deal for a quarter. Chill's house was several blocks away off of Ogeechee Road which kind of explained the tension the day before. We made a drug buy and when Charley brought up a gun, Chill bit.

What you lookin' to get? Chill asked,

A nine, Charley told him.

A'ight, come back this time tomorrow, Chill told him.

The hook was in but now we had to make sure this wasn't some kind of robbery. This side of Ogeechee Road was a little easier to cover. We could have some cover units in the cemetery and some could park up by Frazier Homes and get to Chill's house quickly if we needed to. We did this deal the same way we did every other one but the stakes were higher. We always assumed these guys were armed when they made deals but this time we knew for sure. We were the ones trying to make sure there was a gun involved.

We wired him up and sent him on his way and like all the other times he came right back. We took the recorders and Charley handed us a chunk of Crack and a nine-millimeter High Point pistol. Victory!!!! We had broken our cherry! This was the first gun deal we were able to pull off and we did it without any incident. Smooth as silk. The video was clear and you could identify Chill as the seller, first handing Charley the drugs, pausing and waiting to see what was going to happen, then going inside and coming back with the pistol. We assumed the pause was to make sure there was no buy-bust happening because Chill, a convicted felon couldn't afford to get caught with a gun. The thing is he had been, he just wouldn't find out about it for a while.

I think the deal made Chill kind of nervous though because we would not see him again in the neighborhood and he stopped answering Charlie's calls. Common in this business but I think it was because he had sold a gun and wanted to make sure there was no way it could come back to him.

We were happy to report up the chain of command that we had finally been able to purchase a gun. It was just one gun but man, who would have bought this had we not been able to? What would it have been involved in if we had not taken it off the street? No telling but it was removed directly from an individual who was selling drugs in one of the most dangerous neighborhoods in the city. I have to think it being in an evidence locker was far better than it being in the hands of someone on the street or used to keep someone from "blading a play".

Chill backed off but the word must have gotten out that a gun was sold and that the cops didn't swoop in. Now the approach could be made to others and we found ourselves on the front doorstep of someone who would offer them up.

Open air gun market

Charley rode onto the 500 block of West 38th Street and ran into Donald Baines. Don Don as he was known on the street was a younger, quieter guy on the street. He was always around the other guys but in the background just quietly taking it all in. He ran with Midget and I would see him around the area of 38th and 39th on Burroughs Street but I never saw him far from there. Of course, when I rode through my focus was always on guys like Mhud, Midget, and Trunk but Don Don was never far off and never out front.

Charley struck up a conversation with Don Don and they struck a deal for $100 worth of crack. It went smooth and Charley broached the gun topic.

You got any chrome? Charley asked.

Always, Don Don told him.

*I mean for sale…*Charley pushed.

Don Don said he would see what he could find and they exchanged numbers. Don Don became our point of contact for the next couple of weeks. We would send Charley in and he would get a little crack from Don Don here and there and made a couple of buys from some of the younger guys, if Don Don was not around. Charley's face was now well known in the entire neighborhood and pretty much anyone would sell to him. It was about this time we met Mike Greene who they called "Stinky".

Stinky was a little more notorious than Don Don and was always around Midget and a guy named Trevor Yount. Trevor was a quiet guy but he was by far the most dangerous of the crew. Trevor had "39" tattooed on his face. A "3" on one cheek and a "9" on the other. To say that he was down for his block was putting it mildly. When something went down that involved triggers being pulled, Trevor Yount's name was always one of the ones that came up.

We told Charley to just keep buying dope but not to push the gun issue too far. We wanted to see how it would play. Then one day, he set up a deal with Don Don and he asked,

You still lookin' for a heater? Don Don asked.

Yeah, bruh, I'm always looking, Charley told him, *I work with some dudes that are always looking for throwaways.*

A'ight, Don Don told him, *I got you.*

The next buy we set up was for some crack and a pistol. We didn't specify caliber or anything because as long as it was a functioning firearm being taken out of the hands of any of this crew, we didn't care. Also, we tried to make sure that every time we bought a gun we bought crack at the same time. A 924 (c) calls for an additional 5 years if a gun is used in the furtherance of a drug crime or crime of violence. Since guys like Don Don did not have significant records or histories, because they were young, a 924 (c) case would make sure they didn't get right back out.

Again, because we were inviting a gun into the mix we called out everyone we could to cover. We had units everywhere and gave Charley strict instructions that if the deal got moved anywhere to just ride away. Once he was in, we monitored, but when he got on the block we had to stay out of sight. Sure enough, though, Charley came riding back to our agreed spot, handed us the equipment, crack cocaine, and a .22 caliber pistol. He said it went smooth and described the transaction. When we went back and looked, there was no doubt about how the deal went down. Another gun out of the hands of guys we knew would use them.

We did a few more buys, just like this one, .380, .357 revolver, 9mm, another .22. It was like Don Don was an arms dealer. Each time we would buy, we got crack too. We bought five guns in the next couple of weeks and now Don Don was in serious shit. However, now we had a problem. Things were going so smooth and we had made a case where we could put Don Don away for a lot of years so there was no need to keep buying from him. No reason as far as the prosecution was concerned. I mean in the real world, if you develop a relationship with a guy who sells you guns and drugs at a reasonable price and doesn't give you any shit, why would you shop anywhere else? If we arrested him and charged him with any of the drugs or guns the neighborhood would instantly know who the snitch was and we would be shut down.

Toby and I ran it past Karl Knoche and he agreed there was no need to keep buying from Don Don because it would basically just be running up the score and there was no need for that. Don Don was doing bad things but he was far from public enemy number one. The issue would be, how could we go around Don Don to keep buying from other people? It would be hard to come up with a legitimate reason.

Then something happened that always seemed to happen for Toby and me in a case when we needed it to, we got lucky. Don Don had a warrant for some theft charge from an older case which would violate his probation. I verified the warrant and got a copy of it. I called Josh Hunt and he sent his guys for an easy arrest. Don Don was standing on the corner of 39th and Burroughs with Amhud Dickerson and two of the other usuals when he got scooped up on the warrant. That solved our issue.

Charley went back fishing and because Don Don had not been picked up on any gun or drug charges, no one thought twice about continuing to deal with him. We made a small crack buy off of Trunk just to test the waters. It was smooth and Charley played it off like he didn't know Don Don had been locked up.

The thing is, that didn't stop the guns from coming. Once we had broken that barrier the guys in the neighborhood knew that's what Charley was looking for. After a few small drug buys over the next couple of weeks, Charley ran into Stinky.

You lookin? Stinky asked.

Yeah man but I need something else, Charley told him.

I know Bruh, you need them straps, Stinky replied.

You got me?

Yeah man, I got you. Stinky told him.

They set up a deal and we sent Charley in the next day. Charley rode in and met Stinky at the corner of 39th and Burroughs. As soon as Stinky saw Charley show up he told him to wait and he walked off. A couple of minutes later, Trevor Yount came from the direction Stinky had just gone. Trevor came straight to Charley and handed him a 9mm pistol, Charley handed him the money and Charley rode straight back to us.

That was a little twist we were not expecting but were extremely pleased with. Though Trevor was young he had been indicted on some felonies and was prohibited from possessing a firearm but more importantly, he was a suspect in a murder. This was exactly the kind of guy we were trying to remove from the street and now we were taking guns directly out of his hands. The deal went smooth but Charley came back and said he was wary of this guy. Charley had been in the streets a long time and his sixth sense was telling him something was bad about this guy.

We continued to make deals. With Don Don in jail, Stinky became the point of contact. Charley would set a deal and when Charley rode in Stinky would direct him to the seller. On the next deal, we would get another twist in the direction we wanted to go. Stinky sent Charley to a porch on the 600 block of 39th Street that's when Midget stepped off the porch and served Charley crack cocaine. After all the protesting about how he wasn't doing anything and his name just ringing out in the street, here he was, on camera doing the exact thing I warned him not to do. I was happy to get a strong case against a repeat offender who was exactly the type of guy the neighborhood would benefit from having removed but I was a little saddened because I had extended an olive branch to the kid and he had clearly slapped it away. It was just a reminder to me that this was business, not personal.

We would continue to fish and build a stronger case against Midget and try to get some more guns. The next deal is kind of hard to put in perspective. It was a difficult realization for me and a sure sign the war on drugs that I had been a part of fighting for so many years was simply unwinnable. Charley was headed into the neighborhood and was going to do a deal with Midget. As soon as Midget saw Charley round the corner, he too jumped on a bike and waived for Charley to follow him. To give you an idea of how this goes you have to understand that Cuyler-Brownsville is one of the most patrolled areas in Savannah. There is a patrol car rolling through there all hours of the day, multiple times per hour. This deal was set up almost exactly at noon on a bright sunny day. Unbeknownst to them, they were surrounded by a federal task force of ATF Agents and SCMPD Detectives but here was Midget, a two-time convicted felon, riding a bicycle down the middle of West 38th Street waving to have his customer follow him.

They rode down 38th and turned onto Florence Street where the blocks are misaligned and they turned back onto 38th to continue to Harden St. Midget stopped his bike and one of his associates walked out of a backyard holding a cookie of crack cocaine in his hand and there, in the middle of the street in arguably the most patrolled neighborhood in the city of Savannah at high noon, on a beautiful clear day, they broke off the appropriately sized piece of crack and handed it to Charley. No one paused, looked around, or seemed to worry about being interrupted. They did their business as if they didn't have a worry in the world. I can say in full confidence, that in 2006 when EXPO was on the streets, they would never have felt that comfortable. Soon, we would give them a reason to worry.

I liked doing things from an investigator's position but I have to be honest, I loved being on the street. Riding, seeing what was going on and if the opportunity presented itself, jumping out and doing some work. One day, Toby was tied up with some administrative duties and I was kind of flying solo. I could have and probably should have sat at my desk and done some paperwork that needed to be done but being out on the block was far more appealing.

I checked in with my old partner, SGT Murder…SGT J Murder. It had been a long time since J Hunt and I had ridden in the same car and I thought it might be fun to show his young bucks how shit was done. Hunt's team was a good group. Darren Shroyer, Kevin Fykes, Wendy Terry, Ricky Wiggins, and John Garcia were all up and comers in the department and if they were learning from Hunt and Sean Wilson, the team's other Sergeant, they would be top-notch. Also, they had added Rufus Brown to the lineup when he returned from overseas. I asked Hunt if I could join his group for an hour or so and see if we could drum up any business in CBV, Hunt was all about it. I jumped in his passenger seat and we went after it.

Now, unlike West Chatham's CSU These guys were sharks. We weren't in the neighborhood two minutes before Ricky Wiggins was on the radio and chasing someone, and Wiggins was not a really good-looking guy but he was fast as hell. Seconds later, the guy was in custody. So, not to be outdone, Hunt and I rounded the corner at an old honey hole of ours, 38th and Harden where two young men were standing on the porch of a boarded-up house and began to disperse when they saw us. We stopped to say hello and were greeted by their less than enthusiastic attitudes,

Man, why y'all old heads fuckin with us? One asked as he stepped off the porch.

The other one just kind of tucked himself behind his loud friend and began to slide like he was going to run. Hunt stepped to the side he was moving towards and I ran up the stair to catch his arm as he reached for his waistline. Hunt got the first guy on the ground and I was holding onto the arm that was now trying to pull away from my grasp. Hunt grabbed at his waistband and let me know…

Gun! J Murder reported and we proceeded to escort the young man to the ground. This kid didn't want to fight, he just knew he was fucked and wanted to get away. He was just home from prison and the last thing he could afford was to get caught with a gun…but he did.

I have preached several times about letting small offenses go to get bigger ones and make bigger cases. J Hunt and I have cut people loose with small amounts of marijuana and suspended licenses 100's of times but my rule had always been, no breaks on crack or guns. This kid pled his case and I still can't explain it but something about the way he described his situation and his willingness to give us information made me believe him.

I talked it over with Hunt and we decided we would cut him some slack but that if I needed info, he would answer the call and would tell me or find out what I needed to know. Worst case scenario, we got a gun off the street and had all the guy's information so I could take a warrant if he didn't hold up his end of the bargain. We charged him with obstruction so his partner would see him go to jail but he would be able to bond out on that easily and be back out on the street that day. We exchanged numbers and I put him in my phone as "CBV owes me 1".

It was fun to show the younger guys we still had it and it was a lot of fun to get my heart going again. I enjoyed every second of working the street with J Murder. We would have one more fun run before he left for Chicago.

And then it happened…

We had bought a lot of dope, we were up to about 30 defendants between Caver Heights and Cuyler-Brownsville. We had made an impact in the community in Carver Heights and I had pulled some stats from SARIC. I looked at the crimes that mattered the most to us, Murders, Robberies, and Aggravated Assaults and we even looked at the number of shots fired calls in the neighborhood. We compared the 14 months before S.A.R.G.E. entered Caver Heights and the 14 months while we were operating in the neighborhood. Mind you, Carver Heights is a small neighborhood but the statistical effect was nothing short of remarkable.

From October 2009 until December 2010 there were 21 Aggravated Assaults in Carver Heights alone. That's a big number for a small neighborhood. From October 2010 to December 2011 there were 8. I do not believe in coincidence. During the time that we were kicking in doors and locking up drug dealers Aggravated Assaults in the neighborhood dropped by 61%, Robberies went from 8 to 3, and Murder went from 1 to 0. I have to think the operation had something to do with it. Shots-fired calls were down 48% and drug complaints in the neighborhood was down by more than 61%.

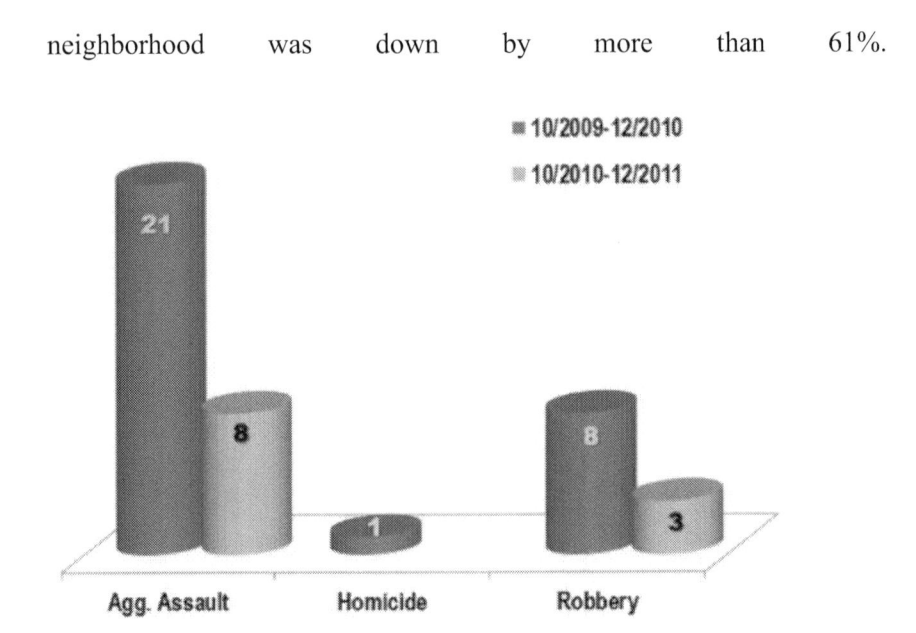

■ 10/2009-12/2010
■ 10/2010-12/2011

Agg. Assault: 21, 8
Homicide: 1
Robbery: 8, 3

Part 1 crime comparison from October 2009 until December 2010 and October 2010 and December 2011 while S.A.R.G.E. was operating in Carver Heights.

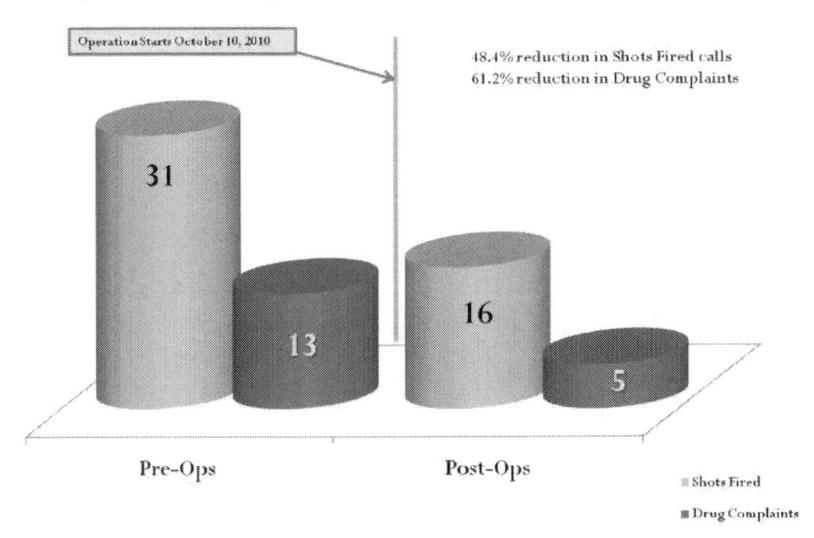

Operation Starts October 10, 2010

48.4% reduction in Shots Fired calls
61.2% reduction in Drug Complaints

Pre-Ops: 31, 13
Post-Ops: 16, 5

■ Shots Fired
■ Drug Complaints

Shots fired and Drug Complaints before and during Operation Ruffian.

Burglary

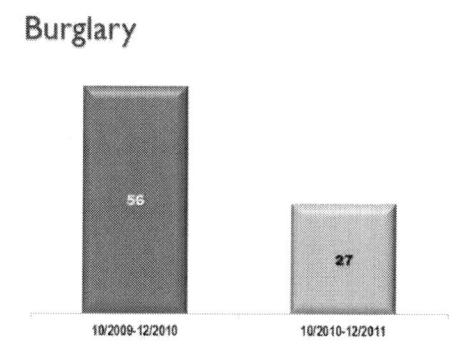

10/2009-12/2010	10/2010-12/2011
56	27

Truthfully, we weren't worried about property crimes but this was just more evidence that the recipe was working.

Toby attended a weekly COMPSTAT meeting where all the Commanders in the Department went over the crime stats and witnessed another anomaly. Captain Phillip Reilly who had taken over command of the West Chatham Precinct went over his part one crime data with the Chief and the numbers reflected a large reduction in the majority of categories. Even his Burglaries were down over 50% during the operation. Which said to me that the bad guys didn't feel safe committing crimes because they were actually afraid of getting caught! Just my opinion but hey...

Captain Reilly did something that very few Commanders in his position would do,

What are you doing to make this happen? The Chief asked

Nothing Sir, it's because of the Task Force, Captain Reilly replied.

They have freed patrol and CSU up to be more proactive and we are seeing the statistical reward.

Toby said he nearly fell over in his seat. He had never seen a Precinct Commander, when given an opportunity to take credit for low crimes stats, completely deflect it and give credit elsewhere. I have always respected and admired Captain Reilly for that and was proud that he felt that way. I didn't know Captain Reilly that well but he was another in a long line of leaders who allowed me to do my job.

A rare chance to feel good in the "what-have-you-done-for-me-lately" world we lived in but we would take it and get back to doing what we did.

We set up another deal with Midget and tried to work a gun into it too. We set it up for the next day and Charley rode in. There were guards posted on the opposite corners of 39th at Burroughs Street and both Midget and Trevor approached. Midget shook hands and handed off some crack cocaine and Trevor came behind and passed off another 9mm and took the money. Again, because a gun was involved, these guys were on high alert looking for police or anything out of the ordinary, unlike just dealing drugs in the middle of the street. They were far more careful and alert in this type of deal but still, they did it and walked away clean. Or so they thought.

Our confidence was at an all-time high and we were hitting on all cylinders. So we got more dope from Midget and Stinky and made a few more attempts at guns. Charley gave Midget a call and tried to arrange to buy two pistols. Midget said he would set it up and off we went. Things had been going so smooth that we rolled in with fewer cover agents. Charley rode in, coming from the southside of the neighborhood, he got to about 40th and Burroughs when Midget came walking up the block and waved him to go towards the middle of the block. Trevor and Stinky were jogging across the street then cut through some houses towards the lane so Charley turned around and rode down the lane.

The transmission on the wire was distorted which was not unusual we could hear voices and chatter but could not really make out what was being said while it was happening but the video would show us clearly how it all went down.

Charley rode into the lane through a cleared lot and behind an old garage. Trevor was there wearing a white baseball hat and was breathing heavily probably from the run they had just made across 40th Street. Stinky approached Charley as Trevor was holding a chrome 9mm pistol with an extended magazine, far nicer than any of the pistols we had bought up to this point.

Damn bruh, that's nice, Charley said,

Yeah? You like that? Trevor answered still trying to catch his breath.

Hell yea, you got that other one? Charley asked.

Trevor, still breathing heavily replied, *Huh?*

Trevor bent over like he was catching his breath and then leaned back as if he needed more air and then he raised the pistol and pointed it at Charley,

Bruh, you know what it is homie, Trevor said with his pistol aimed at Charlie's face.

Stinky approached to get closer and Charley pulled out his buy money, about $500, and handed it to Stinky then put his hand up and said,

It's cool, it's cool, you got it, in full cooperation.

The worst thing you can do in a robbery and what is considered a cardinal sin is buck the jack. Just give your shit up and let it happen. Any resistance, and your only reward was a bullet. We had already let Charley know and he knew from years on the street, that it wasn't worth it. Give it up and live another day and that's exactly what he did.

We didn't know what was going on, we couldn't hear and there was nothing in the garbled transmission that alarmed us but as Charley rode back to meet us he called,

Man, it finally happened, he said calmly.

What happened? I asked.

That boy, Trevor, he robbed me, Charley again calmly reported.

You ok? I asked.

Yeah bruh, just a little shook, Charley said.

We met up and Charley was clearly shaken. He had done everything we told him to do and had handled himself like a professional. I felt like we had let him down because we hadn't swooped in with the cavalry, but in hindsight that might have gotten him killed. Trevor was obviously worked up and wasn't trying to catch his breath because he was tired, it was more like he was anxious and working his way up to do what he had planned to do all along and rob Charley. If we had rushed in at that time, he might have just shot it out, killed Charley, and ran off. We will never know for sure.

We got Charley to relax and made the notifications. I called SGT Gundich and let him know what happened and Toby called GB. Neither were too happy but, hey, this is a dangerous game and in the end, other than being shaken up, no one was hurt. There were a lot of things we could have done better and those things were detailed to us over the next couple of days.

The bright side of it was that this robbery was on video and we would make the clearest case of armed robbery I had ever seen. Robbing a federal informant who is acting on behalf of the government carries the same penalty as if they had robbed or pointed a gun at a federal agent so these guys were in deep shit.

Trevor Yount pointing his gun at Charley.

Devo came to us shortly before the robbery about a rather explosive shooting that occurred at 38th and Burroughs. A lot of the crew we were working with were all suspects but with no witnesses talking and certainly no victims telling Detectives anything because no one had been hit except a few cars. He wanted to know how many of the players we could get off the street before there was retaliation and a war that was escalating between CBV and a gang over around 33rd and Jefferson Street. These guys laid down a lot of rounds from some pretty serious weaponry, 7.62 shell casings meant this was not just pistols being fired back and forth. Captain Adams understood that if we started locking people up on the gun and drugs charges that the operation would be over or at least need a restart.

We had an ethical quandary at this point. We know this business is dangerous and robbery is part of the game but let's face it, we got lucky that it was only a robbery. If Charley had been killed this would have been a lot more than a learning exercise that we could turn into a strong case and teaching point. We had invested a lot of time and a lot of taxpayer money into these neighborhoods.

The drug buys and sales cases were now getting a couple of months old and we couldn't sit on them too long. Most importantly, now we knew definitively we had guys shooting, robbing, and selling guns and drugs that needed to be removed. If we didn't act now and this gang of guys went out and hurt anyone while we could have eliminated the threat then we were assuming a certain amount of liability.

I could hear it now,

*If you could have arrested them before they killed…*And so on.

We all sat down, Devo, Belsky, Gundich, and Toby all agreed now was the time to act. We needed to stop this slide and interrupt the violence that we were watching escalate.

Devo asked how many guys we could take off the block, we could take eleven guys off of that corner immediately plus six more out of Carver Heights. It was also pretty cool to be able to grab 4 or 5 of the guys who were pulling triggers right at the crux of this violence.

I got busy typing arrest warrants for the eleven guys we needed to grab fast to stop the shootings. Trevor, Midget, Don Don, Stinky, and Trunk were all suspects as being part of the mele that occurred at 38th and Burroughs and we could get them all gone. I took the warrants out so we could get these guys arrested and in custody, we would also put the cases that were going federal so we could get them in front of a grand jury and keep them from getting out before bond became an issue. I have never typed so many warrants in my life, between the eleven of them there were almost 137 counts they were being charged with.

Then we put packets together on known locations and information that would help ensure these guys got locked up and couldn't get away. Those packets had everything anyone would need to know about each one of these guys.

When you do a large-scale round-up like this, you need a lot of personnel. We had a few ATF agents, the guys from SARIC and Hunt's CSU knew these guys well but if you are going to round people up, there is no substitute for the U.S. Marshals Fugitive Task Force. We gave them a call and they were more than happy to assist.

We called Tommy Long who was the Deputy Marshal in charge of the task force and was always up for a good round-up. The guys that really made it happen in Savannah at that time though were Geoff Rohrs, Roger Mydel and Andrew Staley. Mydel was SCMPD's Task Force Officer assigned to the Marshals and was the go-to guy for us. When I first came to the department, Mydel was in Homicide and then transferred over. Over the years I couldn't tell you how many guys Mydel wound up grabbing for me but I can tell you, he never let me down. Rohrs was assigned to the Task Force from Parole and was equally as effective. An easy guy to work with and one "Badass Lawman" if you ask around. Staley was from the Chatham County Sheriff's Office and could pick a guy out of a crowd before anyone knew what was happening. If you were after people, there is no question these were the guys to find them.

So, we put an operation plan together, distributed the packets so we would know which team was going to go after which target, and set the date to make it happen. On the morning of the round-up, we met at Central Precinct. The plan was basically to surround the neighborhood and grab any of the targets off the corners where they so religiously posted then move to specific locations for the ones who were not out in the open.

Toby and I would stay back at headquarters and be ready to interview any of the targets as they were picked up. We wanted to be near violent crimes so if any information about murders or robberies came out, they could jump in and take that portion of the interview. We had the briefing and sent the troops out. We waited and the phone started to ring. Midget was first, caught right where I had warned him to stop nearly a year ago. Stinky was next, they woke him out of his bed and there was a gun on his nightstand. Don Don and Trunk were in custody without incident and the guys who stood in the middle of the street and divvied up his crack cookie with Midget came too.

They all started to trickle into HQ while the Marshals continued the hunt. So far Midget was the one I wanted to talk to first.

We sat with Charlton Reagan a.k.a. Midget in the Robbery office at Headquarters. He was not his jovial self but he was also not indignant. Midget and I had known each other on this level for several years and we could talk like men. He sat back in surrender and asked,

What y'all got me for?

Crack, guns and Robbery, I told him.

Man, I ain't jack nobody! He protested.

I told him to chill and explained I had him on video directing a victim to Trevor and Stinky for them to rob. Again, he protested,

Man, I ain't know they was gonna git'em, it was supposed to be a deal, he continued.

I stopped him and said look, man. All of it is on video, weeks of selling drugs and guns, and finally, him waving him over to get robbed.

He leaned forward and looked me dead in the eye,

G, I ain't know they was gonna rob him. I sell drugs man, that's what I do. You got me on that and imma ride but real talk, I ain't know they was gonna jack that boy. On everything I love, you feel me?

Actually, I did. It was entirely possible. I held the warrant for party to the crime of robbery in front of him and tore it up. Midget took responsibility for everything he had sold and as I expected left any of his comrades out of the conversation. I had known him a lot of years and I could say this about him. He was true to the life he was living. It would have been insulting to push him to give up information I knew he was never going to give. He was facing significant prison time and it would all be in the federal system, there was no need to rub it in. I was not really cutting him a break, I was just removing a case where there was reasonable doubt.

I would see Midget one more time before he went to prison, it was at his sentencing hearing where he received 188 months in federal prison. That's 15 and a half years – a long time for a young man but unfortunately, it was necessary to keep a city safe. Toby and I walked past him as Sid, The U.S. Marshal at the courthouse was putting the handcuffs on him for transport. I heard Midget say,

Gimme a second? He asked.

Sid paused as Charlton Reagan reached his hand out to shake mine and said,

You tried to tell me, I appreciate that.

That sticks with me to this day. There is a right way to do the job and I always felt like I did.

I talked to Stinky next and he was less than forthcoming but I really didn't need anything from him. It was all on video. A confession would have only helped him and he was in no mood to help himself, especially since he just picked up another gun charge. Stinky would be sentenced to 12 years.

Don Don didn't want to talk at all because he knew what awaited him. He knew all the guns he had sold and was also enough of a warrior that he wasn't snitching despite the fact he was looking at about 12 years in federal prison, which he got. It could have been a lot worse but Karl Knoche decided there was no need to pour it on and Toby and I agreed. Karl Knoche will always choose justice and fairness over punishment.

The Hunt was on...

We had good luck finding the first five guys and CNT picked up a guy they were looking for too but that left six of our guys in the wind and it wasn't lost on us that the most important, and let's face it deadliest of them all, was still in the wind. Trevor would become our priority.

The Marshals would catch up to a few of our guys pretty quick. Vincent Holbrooke and another corner boy would get snatched up and Chill would get caught on Cornwall Street in Carver Heights of all places.

We were in COMPSTAT and the Chief wanted me to give a brief run down to the command staff of the details of the overall operation. We had made over 50 arrests in the duration of the operation and recovered 37 firearms. Seventeen of the cases were being referred for federal prosecution and we had seized drugs with a street value of over $188,000. We had a lot of things we could point to in the Carver Heights neighborhood that were not enforcement actions and we could definitely point to getting some guns out of Cuyler-Brownsville. I told the story and gave a short presentation and then tried to sit before Chief Lovett could ask me any questions, didn't work but I was happy and able to answer them and give updates on the fugitives still at large. I was ready to leave when Gena Sullivan, the department's Public Information Officer came into the historic squad room and told me that Cedrick Henderson had just been taken into custody in Bulloch County after a three-county high-speed pursuit. He had been in a stolen car which he wrecked and rolled fleeing from Georgia State Patrol and tried to get away on foot but got tased before he could get too far. Gena had done a great job of getting the information on our fugitives out to the local news and setting up some press opportunities that would shine a good light on the operation.

Toby and I got up and headed to the Bulloch County Jail to speak to Ced. Bulloch County jail is in Statesboro, Georgia, you might have heard of it. The Allman Brother's cover of Statesboro Blues is what prompted Toby and Lou to name the storefront operation they did out there the same thing. It's about an hour to the west of Savannah so we had a little ride.

When we got there, Ced had finished being processed and they moved him into an interview room for us. He was disheveled, and had dirt on his clothes, in his hair, and seemed pretty run down. It was an interview I will never forget.

How you doin'? Toby asked him,

He looked at us kind of bothered and replied,

How the fuck does it look like I'm doin? I just got chased, rolled my car, and got tased!

It was hard to be mad at him, he had a point.

Nah man, I ain't mean nothing by it. Just meant are you ok? Toby said.

Yeah man, I'm as good as I'm gonna be. Ced continued.

You know who we are? Toby asked. *Why we're here?*

Yeah, y'all got me, I already know. Ced exclaimed calmly.

We had never met Cedrick Henderson. He was just a guy who was selling crack in a neighborhood we were trying to clean up. He was part of the problem we were trying to correct. As we sat and talked, we learned a lot more about Ced than I ever thought I would care to know and it made me look at things differently for the remainder of my career.

He never even thought about denying that he had sold drugs. He told us that his whole life, that was what he knew. Every man that came into his house and used his mother taught him how to cut, weigh and bag dope and then how to sell it. If he was hungry, he went and sold some dope and got something to eat from the McDonald's or a convenience store nearby. If the water or lights got cut off, he did the same thing. Ced told us he knew it wasn't the right thing to do and that he knew right from wrong but this was just his life. No other option. His mom never registered him in school and he spent his days in the street, hustling. He didn't tell us to try and make us feel sorry for him. He told us to school us on how most of these boys grew up. Ced was particularly worried about Don Don. He told us Don Don was a good kid and would much rather play basketball than be involved in any of the shit that was around him but he had to live in those streets and to survive you had to be hard. It wasn't a choice.

Toby and I listened and we looked back and forth at each other. I knew it was affecting him the same way it was affecting me. It didn't change a thing as far as the charges but I have to tell you, I left that jail with nothing but respect for Cedrick Henderson.

During a homicide investigation later in my career, we would find a video of a couple of these guys talking and joking around. They described how one of them lacked the life skill of being able to order at a restaurant. They didn't order what they wanted, they simply went behind the person in front of them and said,

I'll get what he got... It's another thing that sticks with me to this day.

Over the years, I have been kicked out of many a Facebook thread when discussing crime and poverty. I've debated many tough topics, several of which appear in this book. I have been shut down and shut out many times being told that there is no way I could understand things because I have never been poor or Black. I can tell you this, it's true, I have never been Black and I have never been poor on the level I have just described but believe me when I tell you I have had enough experience in the Black and poor community that I can certainly empathize and I have cared enough to risk my own life and security to protect it.

We were catching up with all the guys we needed to except for one. Trevor was still out there and he was wreaking havoc all over the city. A few weeks after the initial round-up we were getting reports that Trevor was carjacking people in different parts of the city. There was very little intel on the streets about his whereabouts mostly because people were scared to even mention his name, there have been very few names that elicited that type of response in my years in this city.

I got a few reports that no matter how hot things were in CBV, he would still pop in and check on his people. We needed to narrow down a time frame and try and get a bead on a vehicle he might be driving. One night it all came to a head. Trevor had carjacked someone on the southside and units pursued him to West Savannah in a neighborhood known as Sustainable Fellwood. Teams sat and watched the vehicle all night but he never returned to it.

The following morning he carjacked a lady on the East side and we could only assume he was going to hold onto that car, at least for a couple of hours.

There was an old man who lived in the Dips at 38th and Bulloch whom I had talked to for years. He wasn't an informant and hell, he was mixed up in a lot of the little shit that went down over there. This guy always shot me straight because I had cut him some slack on some bullshit over the years. I saw him out and showed him a booking photo of Trevor,

You know this dude? I asked.

Yeah, he cut his hair though. Should be through this morning. Always comes through here.

As I said, this guy always shot me straight.

You seen him lately? I asked.

Yeah, was here this morning, and dropped a dude off in a silver car. The old man said. *Is supposed to be back later this afternoon.*

I got as many specifics as I could but people were starting to move around and this guy definitely didn't want to be seen talking to me. The silver car matched the description of the vehicle Trevor carjacked this morning so I had the tag information and now we knew that his hair was cut low as opposed to the twists that he had worn for the last few months.

We knew, no matter where he was in the city, Trevor, who tattooed "39" on his face would come to the one neighborhood in the world he felt safe, no matter how many cops were looking for him, CBV.

It was a little after 11:00 a.m. and there was only one place to turn. I went to Central Precinct and found the Shift Commander, LT. John Best. I briefed him on the information we had while Toby let Belsky and Gundich know our plan. Toby also called the U.S. Marshals and let them know. LT. Best was my Lieutenant when I first started working in the Downtown Precinct. He had always supported what I did in the street, even as a rookie. We talked a lady off the Talmadge Bridge together and kept her from committing suicide back in 2007. He knew I wouldn't bullshit him. We needed Hunt and his CSU but they were not scheduled to work until 4:00 p.m.

You want me to call them in? LT. Best asked me.

I couldn't even respond. Of course I did but all I could do was nod, so he did. In less than an hour, SGT Hunt and his guys were geared up and in their office.

You have to remember, I had zero rank. I was a patrolman, temporarily assigned to SARIC and attached to an ATF Task Force. Josh and I were the best of friends but he was the Sergeant. George Gundich was my direct supervisor, LT. Best was the shift commander and Toby was an ATF Special Agent who formed the Task Force and each one of them stepped aside and let me run this case.

I briefed Hunt's guys on what Trevor had been doing. He had committed violent and armed felonies in the past 24 hours on top of having warrants for Robbery and Firearm charges. SCMPD's policy dictated at the time the officers would not pursue unless the suspect had committed armed forcible felonies so we had everything we needed to go get him. He had warrants, all for violent felonies, we knew what car he would be in and we knew, eventually, no matter what, he would return to Cuyler-Brownsville. I emphasized that we couldn't let this guy get away because if he did, he would continue to rob and carjack people until someone wound up dead. I told the younger guys there weren't too many opportunities to be able to chase someone and that this was a guy that was worth going until the wheels came off. The old Army Sergeant in me wouldn't let me skip over the safety brief and reminded everyone that even though there was a green light, we still needed to be responsible.

The plan was to surround Cuyler-Brownsville, from Victory Drive to West 37th Street and MLK Boulevard to Ogeechee Road. I told them that we expected him to go to The Dips around 38th and Bulloch Street but they also knew he was always on the corners at 38th and 39th and Burroughs. We would stay on the outskirts until we had a reason to converge. Gundich and the guys from SARIC had already headed to areas north of 37th Street. The Marshals were going to come to Cann Park, just the south of Victory Drive and the rest of us would flank MLK and Ogeechee. We would send Rufus into the neighborhood to see if he could get eyes on Trevor or the vehicle. It was good to have Brown and

Hunt as part of the crew, along with Toby there was nobody on earth I would want more to go into this situation.

I left the briefing full of adrenaline and confidence. I hadn't felt this charged up since my days in Baghdad. We had the right guys in the right places and as much intelligence as we would ever have. It was also very clear to me that I had the full support of everyone in my chain of command. It's days like that where I was truly inspired to do my job.

Toby and I got into the impala after some units had already gone ahead, we left Central Precinct and got to about MLK and Victory when I heard Rufus on the radio. His voice was steady and as calm as it always was,

Suspect vehicle northbound on Ogeechee Road, occupied four times, Brown relayed.

In seconds there was a marked vehicle behind it and less than a second after that, they were hitting the gas and fleeing into the neighborhood.

North on Ogeechee, east on 37th… The radio chatter was constant.

Toby had hit the gas from the moment he heard Rufus' voice. He cut up Burroughs and turned hard left onto 42nd. I'm pointing and trying to give directions as best I can because, next to Josh Hunt, I'm the worst passenger to have in your car when shit is happening. Toby just hit the gas and made the turns. As we were turning north onto Hardin Street from 39th, the call that they had just turned south onto Hardin went over the radio. We were heading straight at them and they were coming straight at us.

I remember two things from this moment as we were barreling right at each other. I remember the driver of Trevor's vehicle's eyes being as big as softballs and Toby very calmly saying,

I ain't turnin'...

As the expression, "Oh Fuck!" went through my mind, the driver made a hard, and I might add skillful, right-hand turn in front of the row house and continued on 38th to Bulloch before turning left onto Bulloch. This turn was not as skillful, but I can tell you that because Toby's driving was good enough to keep us right there with them. Thank God there was enough of a space between the marked vehicle that was behind them and the suspect vehicle for Toby to be able to make that turn.

Trevor's vehicle careened off the far curb and then back left to the opposite curb and came to a sudden stop. All four doors opened and bodies dispersed in every direction. I focused on the rear, driver's side passenger, who ran toward the front of the car, turned hard left, and got into the yard behind the bright yellow boarding house, there was a privacy fence that blocked my view so when I rounded the corner, there was already a uniformed officer headed towards the same opening I was and there were two back doors. Once the runner took that corner I lost sight. It was only logical that they went into one of those doors but they could have also jumped the fence to the east and we would not have seen. I looked over and saw nothing.

The radio chatter continued; 10-95 here, 10-95 there, and one more 10-95 about a block away. We had three of the four in custody…None of them were the one we were looking for.

One of the kids that ran from the car was a 14-year-old. He was running with a revolver in his pants that was the same size as his femur. I got on the radio and got a perimeter set up for about three blocks. Units from all over had come to support. SGT Dan Flood and Downtown's DSO, The U.S. Marshals, people from the ATF office were arriving, Central Precinct patrol units were all in the area. I had walked the block to about 39th and Hardin where Brown was standing. We talked for a minute and both agreed no one could have gotten much further than this without one of us on them and that he had to be within this perimeter. I asked Brown to hold this corner and to make sure no officers moved so we could maintain it.

I went back to the car and there was a pistol on the rear seat. Four people, at least two guns, and three of them in custody. There were cops everywhere north, east, west, and south. This guy couldn't have gotten very far. The clock was ticking and we were looking everywhere, under and on top of every building, behind every fence, into any window we could see in. It started to feel like an eternity. I walked back towards Rufus. Hunt had gotten all the guys that were caught together and began to organize transports to HQ. LT. Best was next to Brown when I got there. The perimeter began to break down. People started to wander and some officers began to get into their vehicles and before I could say a word, LT. Best announced,

Hey! Nobody goes anywhere until I clear you! This isn't just some guy who took off on a bicycle! He yelled.

I remember thinking , *Damn*, and then…my phone rang. I looked down at it and the caller ID read,

"CBV owes me 1"

I answered,

He in the yellow row house, in Mike's apartment, the caller hung up.

I knew exactly which apartment it was because I knew the people in the neighborhood because for months we had been watching, studying, and learning everything we could.

K-9 arrived and coincidentally, so did the property owner. He had heard his property was surrounded by police so he came to see what he could do to help, and probably because he had some experience with this kind of thing, to keep us from kicking in any of his doors.

We had valid arrest warrants and probable cause to believe our guy was in this apartment. From seeing him get to the back yard of this building and disappear, most likely into the back door to a very specific call from a source of information that I had cut some slack a few weeks ago. It was almost poetic. Amanda McGruder, the K-9 handler, and her K-9 Djieno walked up the front stairs with J Murder and me, we used the key to open the front door of the building which brought us to a straight hallway that went straight, all the way to the back door. There were one-bedroom apartments on both sides of the hall. Mike's was the first door to the left as we walked in. We again used the master key to unlock the door to Mike's apartment. We took a tactical position on both sides of the doorway and McGruder issued her commands,

This is the Savannah Chatham Metropolitan Police K-9 Unit, if you do not surrender now, I will release the K-9, come out with your hands up! McGruder instructed.

I heard a muffled voice and saw something moving from underneath the bed and then two hands emerged from under the bed.

I'm good, I'm good. He said calmly.

Hunt jumped in and put the cuffs on and helped the young man to his feet. His hair was short but he still had a 3 on one cheek and a 9 on the other. We had him, Trevor was 10-95. Only 19 years old but we had captured one of Savannah's most dangerous men.

Trevor Yount would plea to all the charges and get sentenced to 180 months in federal prison. About 24 of those were tacked on to his sentence by Judge Moore because, during one of the hearings at the federal courthouse, when Trevor was being detained in the Marshals holding cell, he carved "CBV-39" into a bench that had been there for over 100 years. Judge Moore frowned on that.

Terrence Jackson took this picture of SGT Josh Hunt, Trevor Yount, and I walking out after he was taken into custody. This was the culmination of the best police work I had ever done and I was surrounded by most of the best cops I have ever worked with.

In 2013, I was assigned to homicide, I was walking down the hallway on the third floor near the Robbery office when I caught a glimpse of Charles Sanders being brought into the interview room. Detective Brandon Lord, an old buddy of mine was walking around intently and it was clear he had a case he was working. I peeked my head in the office,

"Hey man, what do you have Chaos in on?" I asked

B Lord told me, *"Bruh, you know him? He's the lookout in a robbery they just did on Styles Ave."*

"He talkin?" I asked,

"Nah man, he's playin dumb," Lord replied. *"Got him on video, wearing a mask right outside the door while his boy hit the lick".*

Now, I don't like to get involved in other people's cases but I KNEW I could help on this. I didn't even need to see the video. I asked Lord if he would let me talk to Chaos for a few minutes to see if I could get him to be a little more cooperative. I hadn't seen Chaos since that day at the MLK Parade but I know I had made an impression and I also knew he saw what S.A.R.G.E. had done in his neighborhood.

B Lord said *"Have at'em"*

I walked into the interview room, shirt and tie, you know, the homicide get up and sat across from Chaos, when he looked up and saw me I could see instantly he remembered me. He had the ultimate "oh shit" look on his face.

"You remember me? I asked

He just nodded.

"Why you here?"

He started all the usual bullshit, "they grabbed me up for no reason", "I don't know why they're fuckin with me", blah blah blah. I cut him off immediately.

"Bruh, I've been lookin at pictures of you and your boys for years. 1000's of pictures of nothing but you. Detective Lord showed me that video with you in that mask and I told him exactly who it was. Stop bullshitting and tell the man what the fuck happened."

Chaos paused and gave B Lord the story.

It's not always what you know or even what you can prove, sometimes just being in their head can get you what you need to make a case. The type of intelligence we had in Carver Village and Cuyler-Brownsville put us ahead of the curve which isn't an easy place to get in police work. The roadmap worked in 2010-2012 and can easily work again if a department doesn't lose all its assets first. There are consequences for weak leadership and I think we are seeing that as a nation and I know we are seeing it in the city of Savannah, Georgia.

Acknowledgments

I would like to remember Aulmon Giles who served the Savannah Police Department for 43 years. He was a mentor to so many including me and had such an unassuming way of helping younger officers whether they knew they were being helped or not. He had a respect for the Law Enforcement profession that I have never seen in anyone else. I never heard him refer to us a cops, to Detective Aulmon Giles, we were policemen. Rest well Sir, you've earned it and we'll take it from here.

This book could not have been written, the story could not have been told and my life would mean less were it not for my friend and brother, Toby Taylor. Thank you for always bringing me along for the ride. I am forever in your debt.

I want to again acknowledge my friend and mentor, Greg Capers. This operation wouldn't have happened, for me at least if you hadn't done what you always do. Look out for the next guy. When I look at anything that I consider a success in my career, you are directly connected to it. Thank you for always believing in and looking out for me.

Terrence Jackson, you my brother are one of a kind. Thank you for always being by my side.

Retired Chief Willie Lovett, thank you for always allowing me to do my job and supporting me when I did.

Captain George Gundich, thanks for always doing the right thing by your officers. You are appreciated on levels that probably won't matter to you until you are an old man…and you are pretty close. I learned from you from the day I stepped into the Downtown Precinct and I won't ever forget what you have done for me. Thank you.

Rufus Brown and Josh Hunt, you two are the best I ever saw play the game. I'm honored to know you both.

Lou Valoze, this has got to be our year. I never have to check my back because I know you are always there. Love you Brother.

George Belsky…I don't know how to thank you, this is the best I've got.

Chris Bayless, having you as a part of this is a greater honor for me than you will ever know. Thank you my brother.

To my friend and the most honorable man I know, Karl Knoche. Thanks for being a pro and thank you for not giving up on me.

To Judge James Bass and Judge Louisa Abbott. Thank you for understanding and supporting what we were doing. It would not have been possible to accomplish the things we did without your support.

The ATF Savannah Field Office, thanks for always giving me a second home and for all the lessons along the way.

The Georgia Bureau of Investigation, The US Marshals Service, Savannah Probation and Parole, SCMPD S.W.A.T., and K9 Units…I hold you all in the highest regard.

The rest of Sgt Hunt and Sgt Wilson's CSU, Wiggins, Fykes, Shroyer, Terry, and Garcia, thank you for being good at what you do.

To every female officer I have ever served with, especially Jenessa Stalter, Sam Uribe, Shinita Young, Tiffany Saytanides-Manuel, Kimberly Laff, Amanda McGruder, Lara Hannegan, Casondra Lawton, Karen Ryan, Ladonna Clark, Shamonica Badie. My career was enriched by having worked with each of you. My apologies in this book are as sincere as I can be. Thank you all.

To everyone in SARIC that made my job easier and more enjoyable. Elleby, Carter, SGT Mac, Captain Wiley, Ronda, Kristin, Gianna, Faith, Zee, and…thank you so much.

To the current members of the Savannah Police Department, thank you for continuing to do your duty with honor and integrity. I no longer wear a badge but I stand behind you, always. Even if you don't agree with my approach I want you all to know that my only intention in writing this book and speaking out is to make your job easier and hopefully get you what you need to effectively conduct your mission of keeping us all safe. I am in your debt.

Jason Usry, man, where the hell would we be without you? Thank you, and I wish you all the continued success the world can bring you, my brother.

Bob and Maureen Eason, for your unbelievable and continued support.

To Joni "The Booklady" and Chris - Thank you both so much for all the help and support you give authors in our city and all over. You're the best.

The ladies at E. Shaver Booksellers - Thank you for your continued support.

To my brothers and sisters from the mighty 529th Military Police Company "Honor Guard". My time and service with you all probably shaped me as a professional more than any other period in my life.

I have to admit, I enjoyed writing this book much more than I enjoyed writing my first. I was in an entirely different state of mind, mostly because this time, I'm in love. My fiancé has made this journey so much more tolerable. We will be married shortly following the release of this book. To my Kristi, thank you and I love you dearly.

Made in United States
Orlando, FL
07 June 2022